COMPLETE AS ONE

COMPLETE AS ONE

Elizabeth-Ann Horsford

HODDER AND STOUGHTON
LONDON SYDNEY AUCKLAND TORONTO

British Library Cataloguing in Publication Data

Horsford, Elizabeth-Ann
   Complete as one.—(Hodder Christian
   paperbacks).
   1. Single people—Religious life
   I. Title
   248.4   BV4596.55

ISBN 0 340 41444 8

DEDICATION

I dedicate this book to the memory of my mother who spent many years on her own as a widow, and to all my single friends.

I should also like to express sincere thanks to all those who read the manuscript and made helpful comments. Very special thanks to Jean Watson, herself a writer, for her invaluable help in painstakingly editing and correcting the manuscript and for all her encouragement. Also to Terry McCauliffe, who had the exacting job of typing and re-typing the manuscript, which she did with her customary good humour.

CONTENTS

FOREWORD

My boss had just returned from another speaking tour in the USA. We were sitting in his small office at Hildenborough Hall over coffee.

'She started out life in the theatre.'

'Oh! really,' I said.

'And was a debutante too,' Peter added. It was Monday morning and I had been away on a weekend mission. In my weariness I momentarily lost the thread of his story. I sheepishly said, 'I'm sorry, but remind me who you said this woman was?'

'She's the one I have invited to join the team.'

I'm not sure whether my face betrayed me, but I started slightly inside at the thought of some kind of classy actress joining our ranks. I was about to ask Peter if he was certain she was a Christian, when he divulged some further helpful information.

'She was Vice Principal of a Missionary Training College here and had worked with several organizations, including the Navigators, in different countries.' He leaned back in his creaky chair and expressed satisfaction with the situation on three counts. 'I am sure the Lord is in this. She will bring a lot of new gifts into the team. You and Sue will enjoy working with her.'

He was right. Elizabeth-Ann joined us and God has used her ministry in a powerful way which continues to develop across Britain and in other countries. Her successful seminars, conferences and numerous speaking engagements, have touched many lives. I am not surprised to see a publisher now bringing her ministry to a wider public.

This book is a must for anyone – single or married. I wish I had read it when I was single; I'm glad I have read it as a married man. The great thing about Elizabeth-Ann's writing is that it is honest and realistic, as well as spiritual and biblical. She understands the gamut of feelings we experience and can lead us from that point to where we need to be – not dominated by feelings but giving priority to God's blue-print for our attitudes and lifestyle.

Every Christian person should read this book because its underlying message is the secret of a fulfilled life for any Christian, whatever their situation. Understanding and living with yourself, trusting the God who is in control of your circumstances, having the wisdom to avoid being conned by the traps of today's social environment, and being decided to keep your mind on a course which is in line with what God wants – these are all vital to us. Too often this quality of life eludes us and we are then less than we could be.

Elizabeth-Ann's understanding, sympathetic and yet determined approach is exactly the recipe most of us need – because it is, in fact, Jesus's approach.

I always find I can take advice, spiritual counsel and practical hints fairly easily from people who practise what they preach. This is probably one of the most compelling things about the book for me personally. I have worked in a team with Elizabeth-Ann for more than five years. Without doubt she is one of the most fulfilled people I know.

Max Sinclair
May 1987

INTRODUCTION

Brian turned to me with a smile. 'You know what I appreciate most about June? She is so satisfied with Christ.' I had never heard anybody make a statement like that before. But as I thought about it I realised it was true. My friend June was deeply satisfied with Christ and it showed so clearly.

That phrase 'satisfied with Christ' stuck with me and challenged me. I was 21 at the time, and had been converted three years before. Many of my friends were getting engaged and married and of course I was happy for them. What did bother me, though, were the comments I often heard made about them. 'Have you seen Mary? She is radiant. She's just got engaged.' 'John's a changed man. He's fallen in love.' 'I've never seen Jean so happy now she's getting married.' All these friends were Christians and I began to question in my mind why they had to wait to get a partner before they could experience the joy and fulfilment that Christians should have. So often I had seen rather miserable-looking people walking around who called themselves Christians. And it had for a while put me off coming to know the Lord. One day, soon after Brian's comment, I found myself praying, 'Lord I don't want to marry until I have learned to be satisfied with you.' I felt jealous for the honour of God and as I told Him so that was the prayer He put into my heart.

It hasn't always been easy. A few years after I prayed that prayer I received a proposal of marriage from a fine Christian I had known for years. I turned him down. Not because of that prayer but because I knew he was not the one for me.

How many unhappy marriages there have been because people have rushed into them thinking this might be their only chance. He later became a happily married man, to the right person.

Later I met someone with whom I fell in love. I believed, and so did several of my friends at the time, that he was the one for me. But in the end it was not to be. It was a heartbreaking experience, but God reminded me that I had said at the beginning of my Christian life that I wanted to obey His will whatever the cost 'even though I may kick and scream', and I was certainly kicking and screaming then. But I had had sufficient proof by then that God's way is the best and I have certainly proved it since.

The overall aim of this book is to show that God has proved Himself to me to be able completely to satisfy and fulfil my life as a single person, and my prayer is that you will find this true for you, too. He is the same Lord.

I pray that this book will be a blessing to all single people, men and women, whether divorced, widowed, or who have never married.

I feel there are some fundamental facts which are important for us to consider, and which I personally have found to be key factors in my life. I refer to such things as knowing who is at the controls of your life; having a good Biblical sense of self-worth; facing but not fearing the problems of singleness; and how you can make the most of your life as a single person.

1

WHO IS AT THE CONTROLS?
(The sovereignty of God in daily life)

'I do hope you marry one day, but you may not, because there are so many more Christian women than there are men.'

'You were called into nursing and your friend got married? You really came off worse in that deal.'

Both of these remarks, said at different times by different people, hit me where it hurts. The first made me think that I would always be the victim of statistics and that God really was unable to do anything about it. The second remark made me feel that for some reason God must have it in for me and whereas He did nice things for others He didn't intend to do them for me. Later on I came to realise that both were untrue. One of the things that helped me to that realisation was gaining a greater awareness of God, derived, I think, from my parents, who were God-fearing people, especially my mother. As a child I had been brought up to go to church and Sunday school and had been taught about the goodness of God and how He looked after us. This was just head knowledge to me at that time, and led me, erroneously, to believe that tragedies happened to other people, not me. So my first thought when finding myself aged 8 in a shattered car which had been in a head-on collision was that God must have been asleep. But God, we are told, neither slumbers nor sleeps (Ps. 121:4).

PERPLEXING PROBLEMS

I have many unanswered questions, but looking back now I can see that God was not asleep. I would never say that God sends accidents, cancer and the many other evil things we see in our world: murder, rape, wars and such. These things have come into the world because of the sinfulness of man and the wrongful exercising of his free-will. But this does not mean that God is not in control of His world. Far from it. But He does allow certain things to happen, even things that seem evil. Job is a great example of this. God allowed Satan to touch his possessions, his children and then his body, but he was not allowed to take his life. God wanted to make Job a test case of one who continued to trust God in spite of his disasters. He may have cursed the day he was born, but he never cursed God.

At the age of 17 Joni Earekson-Tada dived into the shallow waters of Chesapeake Bay and broke her neck. Couldn't God have stopped that happening? A student I know of was unable to sleep because the weather was so humid. He went to the college baths in the middle of the night and climbed on to the highest diving-board in the moonlight. He was about to dive when the moon shone through the window and the reflection of a cross from the window frame fell across the pool. He was so struck by this that he climbed down and went to look over the edge of the pool. It had been drained of water. To use his own words, 'I was saved by the cross!' Why him and not Joni? God knows.

Joni's accident left her a quadriplegic, but her books and films have helped thousands around the world. She believes, as I do, that God is in control.

Who has measured the waters in the hollow of his hand, or with the breadth of his hand marked off the heavens? Who has held the dust of the earth in a basket, or weighed the mountains on the scales and the hills in a balance? Who has understood the Spirit of the Lord, or instructed him as his counsellor? Whom did the Lord consult to enlighten him, and who taught him the right way? Who was it that taught him knowledge or showed him the path of understanding? (Isa. 40:12-14).

The answer to all these questions is 'no one'. There was no one needed to teach God wisdom, understanding or knowledge. He Himself is the source of all wisdom, understanding and knowledge.

'Surely the nations are like a drop in a bucket; they are regarded as dust on the scales; he weighs the islands as though they were fine dust' (v.15).

That verse reminds me of a plane journey I once took. The problems I was facing at that time suddenly assumed their right size as I looked down on those tiny houses, cars and people.

In our world today we are sometimes frightened by the superpowers as we hear them shouting at one another, and we sense war clouds gathering. Do these rulers really have total power? Verse 23 tells us that God 'brings princes to naught and reduces the rulers of this world to nothing.' He has no equal as we see in verse 25: '"To whom will you compare me? Or who is my equal?" says the Holy One.'

He is unique and all-powerful and we are like grasshoppers before Him. But the other side of the coin is that God loves us and cares for the individual. 'Lift up your eyes and look to the heavens: who created all these? He who brings out the starry host one by one and calls them each by name. Because of his great power and mighty strength not one of them is missing' (v.26).

Think of the billions and billions of stars, some of which man hasn't even discovered yet. God knows them all by name. If that is so, it really isn't incredible that He knows each one of us by name, and where each of us is, and what each of us needs at any given time. God may be withholding marriage at this time to achieve a greater purpose in us, or He may see that we are not ready.

GOD DOES CARE

There was a time in my life when I was doing a very boring job. I was working with a Christian organisation and receiving training at their headquarters, I thought, for a responsible position of ministry among women. Guess what job I was assigned? Typing receipts in the finance department. All day, every day, for weeks, and no mistakes allowed. I was sure some mistake had been made and that God had forgotten me. So I reminded Him of where I was and asked Him to get me out of there soon. He reminded me that He had not forgotten me and made it clear that He had lessons to teach me in the job. When the right time came He moved me, but I'm grateful for the lessons I learned there. Many people would echo the sentiment of verse 27 of Isaiah 40:- 'Why do you say, O Jacob, and complain, O Israel, "My way is hidden from the Lord; my cause is disregarded by my God"?'

God does not care about me, or know my situation. He is too great to bother or care. But that is the wrong implication. The right implication comes in verse 28 which tells us that God is too great *not* to care. 'Do you not know? Have you not heard? The Lord is the everlasting God, the Creator of the ends of the earth. He will not grow tired or weary, and his understanding no-one can fathom.'

The Bible tells the story of a young girl, Esther, beautiful and loved by all who knew her, who was taken from her home and her loved ones to become the wife of a man she had never seen and of whom she might have been justifiably afraid. He was a king, and a king of a foreign and pagan power. How easily she could have rebelled against her unjust lot. But nowhere in her story is this evident. On the contrary she maintained the sweet attitude that had endeared her to her friends, and the submissive spirit which had commanded the respect of her guardian, and as a result she rose to a position where God was able to use her in one of the most dramatic moments in history.

She had come to the kingdom 'for such a time as this' and because of her actions and prayers was used to save her people, the Jews, from total destruction.

Certainly God would have heard and had compassion on the tears and anguish she must have experienced when taken away from home and loved ones to satisfy the lust of a sensual and indulgent man. Yet God had a greater plan, and Queen Esther has gone down in history as a saviour of the Jewish people, and a woman renowned for her courage and availability to God.

DID GOD SEND THIS?

One of the questions that often torments our minds in times of adversity is: 'Is this trouble from God or an attack from Satan?'

To return to the book of Job, it gives us a wonderful picture of God in total control even over Satan, to whom he gives limited authority to test Job. God was going to prove for all time to Satan and to mankind that He is in control of the world and the affairs of men, and that it is possible for a man to love God for Himself alone and not just for what He gives him. Job was tested by financial disaster, the loss of all his children and by severe illness. Yet through all this he hung on to God and came out on top. Chapter 1 of Job is really the clue to the whole book. God allowed Satan to test Job – please note that He set the limits beyond which Satan could not go – yet look at Job's response:

... 'The Lord gave and the Lord has taken away; may the name of the Lord be praised' (Job 1:21).

We learn from this that although Satan brought all these calamities on Job, God had ultimate control and Satan's power had limits.

WHAT ABOUT ME?

You may feel, 'It's all very well for people in the Bible, but what about me and my life today? Does God really care about me and know about my problems?' Let me give you a personal answer. Many things have happened to me in my life. Some of those things have been pleasant and some very unpleasant and perplexing. Yet I am increasingly convinced that God knows what He is doing and wants the best for me.

This does not mean that I understand exactly why God does or allows certain things. An elderly friend told me that one day her grandson said to her, 'Granny, you're quite old, aren't you?' This fact 'Granny' acknowledged. Then with the blatant honesty of children the boy continued, 'You'll soon be dead, won't you?' My friend replied, 'Yes, I expect I will.' 'Well,' the young philosopher said, 'I know what you are going to ask God when you get to heaven. You're going to ask, "God, who made you?" and God will answer "That's not for you to know."'

We know that God had no Creator, but there are many things that God does not tell us. But He does reveal what we need to know.

'The secret things belong to the Lord our God, but the things revealed belong to us and to our children for ever, that we may follow all the words of this law' (Deut. 29:29).

Does the fact that God is in control mean that it doesn't matter what I do because God will do what He wants, anyway? Again the answer is, No. Actions do have consequences and God does allow us to exercise free will and then reap what we sow. If I drive recklessly there is every likelihood that I will have an accident. If I constantly abuse my body I am likely to shorten my lifespan. But God can still turn anything we experience to good account and achieve His purposes while allowing us His gift of freedom.

God's greatest purpose for anyone is that he or she will become more like Jesus. And it is often through adverse circumstances that God brings that about. It isn't that God singles out an individual and says, 'Mary could learn to be more patient if I put her through such and such a nasty experience.' The fact is, in this fallen world there *is* disease and accidents *do* happen. These are all directly, or indirectly, the result of sin in the world and its effects on nature. God is still in control, but He chooses to allow the course of this world to continue, often without intervention, while doing all that he can, without using force, to bring us to the point of handing over the control of our lives to Him. He longs to help us to realise our fullest potential and lead purposeful lives. He waits and works in this way because He longs for 'all men to be saved and to come to a knowledge of the truth' (1 Tim. 2:4).

What about those whose lives are under His control, who are fully committed to Him in discipleship? Why does God allow bad things to happen to them? Once again, it is true that these people, too, are living in a world of sin where disease and accidents are rife, and no one is singled out for escape however good they may be. God can use adversity to refine and purify that life, producing Christ-like qualities that can be used in blessing to many.

REFINED FOR BLESSING

Precious stones are refined in fire to rid them of impurities. The fire is never too hot nor kept on longer than is needed. At the right moment the jewel is taken out and its crystal clearness and real beauty is seen. If, in the midst of adversity, we can ask God to use it for His glory in our lives in making us more like Him it will not have been wasted. Surely this is what we mean when we sing the chorus:

> Make me like a precious stone
> Crystal clear and finely honed
> Life of Jesus shining through
> Giving glory back to you.

Adverse circumstances, though, do not automatically do good in our lives. Psychologists tell us that it isn't so much *what* happens in our lives that is important but the *way* we react to what happens.

CONTRASTING REACTIONS

A young missionary was kidnapped by bandits and raped. Some time after her release, a fellow-missionary asked her, 'What did you learn from that terrible experience?' 'Nothing. Nothing. It was just terrible,' was the answer. Our hearts go out to that young woman who endured probably the worst experience any woman can undergo. Yet all she was left with was bitterness and resentment.

In contrast there is the story of Helen Roseveare. I remember hearing her speak at a large meeting in London when she told of her experience of being raped and how she felt God had used it to teach her some valuable lessons concerning her own pride, which had caused so much difficulty on the mission field. She readily admitted that she had been a great trial to her fellow-missionaries and superiors, but as a result of allowing God to use this terrible experience to mould her, the blessing of her life has been far-reaching.

The missionary who asked her colleague what she had learned from her traumatic experience, was a woman with whom I had the privilege of working for eight years. Her

name was Audrey Wetherall Johnson, founder of Bible
Study Fellowship. Before I met her, she had lived for nearly
three years in a Japanese concentration camp, suffering
greatly herself as well as witnessing the suffering of others.
Through it all, however, she experienced the close presence of
God and He was preparing her for her life's work. Following
her release from camp, and some further years of privation
under communist rule in China, she found her way to the
United States, ostensibly to visit a friend for a short while.
But God had other plans and the Bible Study Fellowship was
started – an organisation which now has hundreds of classes,
in the United States, Britain and Australia. Thousands of
men and women have been through the five-year Bible course
and hundreds have become true or more committed
Christians whose personal and family lives have been
transformed.

So, why do some people develop new qualities and learn
important lessons through adverse experiences while others
do not? I believe it is a matter of personal choice and attitude.
One of the things that I often heard Miss Johnson say was,
'Don't waste your suffering.' When something bad happens
to us – an unhappy childhood, parental rejection, a handicap,
accident, divorce, bereavement or anything else – we can
choose to be resentful and bitter or choose to be accepting
and forgiving. If we believe that God knows all about what we
are going through and wants the best for us, we can and
should move from a negative to a positive attitude and thus
not waste our suffering.

Once when I was in hospital recovering from major
surgery, my minister visited me and gave me the verse; '"For I
know the plans I have for you," declares the Lord, "plans to
prosper you and not to harm you, plans to give you hope and
a future"' (Jer. 29:11). This was a great encouragement to me
in the wearisome convalescence that followed and I have been
proving its truth ever since.

Many single people, who have never been married,

seriously wonder if God does have good plans for them, or if it is really true that He will not withhold good things from them as it tells us in Psalm 84. They feel they have been hard done by, or that they are victims of statistics. Is God really stumped by statistics? How laughable! I have seen two people come together in marriage from the opposite ends of the world. Sometimes singles can become bitter about their single state and their lives become so unhappy and unfulfilled.

THE INFECTION OF BITTERNESS

Hanging on to bitterness is the greatest hindrance to the good that God intends for us. It is spiritual infection. Just as infection has to be removed from a wound before it can heal, so bitterness has to be rooted out before emotional healing can take place. Stitching a cut finger before the infection has been removed is useless and even dangerous, so prayers, tears and turning over a new leaf are no substitute for dealing with and letting go of bitterness, anger and an unforgiving spirit. If these things are not dealt with in the end they can cause serious problems. Unresolved conflicts tend to tear us apart, and must be dealt with.

Corrie ten Boom, who with her father, sister and brother suffered so terribly in a Nazi concentration camp, and alone survived the ordeal, tells how some years later she felt the Lord telling her to go back to Germany to speak of His love for the German people – in itself a hard thing for her to do. One day she had just finished speaking at a meeting in Germany when she noticed a man coming up to her from the back of the hall. He obviously had not recognised her, but she instantly recognised him as one of the guards who had been most cruel to her and her sister. As he reached her he put out his hand and explained that now he was a Christian he was asking forgiveness of everyone who had been in a concentration camp.

Corrie was smitten. How could she forgive this man after what he had done, not so much to her but to her sister? She had visions of his brutality as she stood there silently looking at him. It was impossible to forgive, she thought. Yet she knew that God had called her so to speak about the love of God, above all that Christ had suffered on the cross out of love, and she knew she had to forgive or go home, defeated. So in her heart she asked the Lord to fill her with love and forgiveness and by a sheer act of will she put out her hand to take his. As she did so, she recounts, peace and joy filled her heart and she was truly able to say she had forgiven him. She was free. The wound could now heal as the infection had been removed. But it was an act of the *will*, not of the emotions. If she had waited until she felt like it she would have probably waited for ever. Who would 'feel' like forgiving in a situation like that? But she knew she had to. '... if you do not forgive men their sins, your Father will not forgive your sins' (Matt. 6:15).

Perhaps there is someone who has deeply hurt you. A parent, teacher, friend, boyfriend, girlfriend. Or you feel angry with God because of a situation in your life that you want changed. Perhaps you are resentful that you are single; bitter that you have never been asked out or that the right person has never come along, and you are angry with God because of this. Or maybe you are suffering from the deep wounds of rejection caused by a divorce or separation, or by the pain of being widowed, asking, 'Why did God take my husband?', 'Why did God take my wife?'

DEALING WITH BITTERNESS

I should like to suggest some steps you could take to be free from bitterness and resentment.

First, admit your feelings to God. Don't pretend you don't feel that way if you do. Many Christians do not acknowledge to themselves, let alone to God, that they are angry and resentful, because it is 'unspiritual' to feel that way. But we must face facts. Unacknowledged emotions can harm us. We need honestly to admit to ourselves, and to God, how we feel. Whether we later go on to express our feelings to the one involved (when our own heart is right about it and our attitude forgiving) is our choice which should be made on the basis of whether it will further or hinder God's purpose.

Second, ask God's forgiveness for your wrong attitude of anger and resentment. You may feel you have a right to feel angry and resentful. That person was wrong (hurtful, unjust, untruthful, etc.). Perhaps so, but their wrong-doing to you is their problem and God will deal with them over it in His time. *Your* problem is the anger and resentment. When you are angry and resentful or bitter towards someone, you are the one who is hurt most. The person to whom these feelings are directed may not even know or care. But you are being eaten up inside. As you give these feelings to God, who was willing to forgive those who tortured and crucified His Own Son, He will forgive you and set you free from the inner turmoil of that anger and resentment.

Third, thank Him for the fact that the person or circumstance which caused your suffering is under His control and He can and will bring good into your life through this situation.

Fourth, commit yourself afresh to God, telling Him that you promise to co-operate with Him in all that He wants to do in your life in the future.

One of God's great purposes is to make us holy and one day to present us without blemish, like His Son, Jesus Christ (Rom. 8:29). The refining process is never pleasant, and sometimes might lead us though the fires of suffering. Our natural feeling tell us that it's because God does *not* love us that we are going through this terrible time. In fact, it is because God *does* love us so much that he will not settle for anything less than this high purpose for us, of making us like Christ. If we will allow Him to burn away the dross of bitterness and resentment, then God's highest purpose for us can be achieved.

The fact that we are single may be because God has something to teach us in our single state that we could never learn if we were married. Or that He desires to use us in ways we could never be used if we were encumbered with the responsibilities of married life. I shall be developing this later! But my main purpose in this chapter has been to help us realise that God is in control. He is not taken by surprise and He does have a good and loving plan for us if we are willing to let Him show us.

As we shall see in the next chapter, we are people of great value and infinite variety and God is able to use us within the context of our varied personalities.

2

YOU ARE A PERSON OF DIGNITY AND WORTH
(The biblical concept of self-worth)

How much are you worth?

A friend of mine had a beautiful picture in his home. After a number of friends had commented on it, and assured him that they thought it was of great value, he decided to take it to an art dealer for an expert opinion. He carefully wrapped up the painting and walked proudly into the dealer's feeling sure that, having seen it, they would give him the red-carpet treatment! Imagine his disappointment when, after fifteen minutes of careful scrutiny, the art dealer said, 'Sorry, sir. We are not interested in this painting. We don't know the artist and we don't feel the painting is of any value.' My friend wrapped the painting up again and quietly left feeling somewhat deflated. Returning home he re-hung his picture, because it did have value to him and his family. Then he made a very significant observation: that value is often placed on something by the importance of the one who created it and the amount anyone is willing to pay for it.

That story spoke volumes to me about the worth of the individual. God created you. God Himself. No one is greater. God gave His only Son for you. There never was nor ever will be a greater price paid for anything than that – the death of God's Own Son for you and for me.

In the light of these facts, how much are you worth? You may say, 'In spite of knowing that God created me and Christ died for me, I still don't feel worth anything. You don't know me and how worthless I really am.' Many people talk like that, and many more think like that although they might never admit it.

FEELINGS OF WORTHLESSNESS

So why do so many people feel so worthless? Some singles may feel unworthy because they are single – that they must have something wrong with them. 'If only I were better looking; had a better personality; had more sex appeal,' and all the things the world wrongly tells us, erroneously, are important, 'then I would not still be single.' But none of these things has anything to do with our worth (or, for that matter, necessarily with the fact that we are single). If we are focusing our attention in the right direction, namely to our standing before God, these things need not affect our *sense* of worth either.

But not only singles are affected in this way. In a survey made in the United States it was discovered that the major cause of depression among married women was a low self-image. And surely it doesn't only affect women but men too. Men have trouble accepting themselves and feeling good about themselves and this shows, among other things, in their attitude to women and particularly as far as their attitude to the role of women is concerned. A man with a poor self-image, perhaps because of a dominant mother, will feel especially threatened by an efficient women working alongside him.

So where do all these feelings begin? Much of the way we feel about ourselves is shaped by childhood experiences and the expectations of others. 'My mother always told me I was stupid.' 'I could never measure up to the expectations of my father. I know I disappointed him.' 'My teacher said I was a dunce.' We can also be affected by non-verbal communication. One woman, who had had many breakdowns and severe psychological problems, told me that her mother completely ignored her. She recounted how one day, when she was an adult, someone who had come into a room where she was, noticed her after a while and said, 'I didn't know you were here.' A very innocent remark which would have been quickly dismissed by a healthy mind. But this woman, who had suffered so deeply by being ignored, said, 'That is the story of my life. It's as though I don't exist.' Her mother's treatment of her had done much harm.

Our childhood experiences can be very powerful in giving us, or failing to give us, a sense of our own worth.

So how can we gain a sense of self-worth if we do not have it? First I think we need to understand, believe and receive some basic facts.

WE ARE FEARFULLY AND WONDERFULLY MADE – PHYSICALLY

When God finished all His creation, including the crown of His creation, man and woman, we read, 'God saw all that he had made, and it was very good' (Gen. 1:31). When we consider the intricacies of the human body, the millions of cells, the brain, the circulatory and nervous system, the workings of the heart and lungs, we can only marvel at the wonder of God's creation and agree with George Gallup that to think we came about in any haphazard way would be a statistical monstrosity. Each person has sixteen different characteristics in their fingerprints. Even identical twins have their differences!

Because of sin having entered the world, there are many imperfections in us, not only in character but in looks. Some, sadly, are born with birth defects, or handicaps. But these in o way affect our personal worth.

Mary was born with a facial disfigurement which ecessitated the removal of her eye at an early age and many perations to remove recurring growths on her forehead. 'art of her skull was very thin so any bump to her head aused serious bruising and internal bleeding. Cold weather nd loud noise affected her very badly and much of the winter he would be confined to her home. Childhood was hard, and dolescence worse as she watched her friends being invited ut. When I met her she had retired, having had an active and ulfilling career in institutional management in both schools nd hospitals and in her spare time working with blind eople. The thing I noticed about Mary was her courage, oyfulness, head held high and lack of self-pity. Because of hese qualities all who knew her seemed quickly to forget the isfigurement. Even now I don't think about that when I hink of her, but her vibrant life and love for people and for he Lord. She knew she was a person of worth. Because of hat she gave courage and hope to many.

Accepting the way God made you, physically, is an ngredient in a true sense of self-worth.

VE ARE FEARFULLY AND WONDERFULLY MADE – EMOTIONALLY

Ve are not all alike in looks and personality. The world vould be very dull if we were. Not only do we have the bodily lifferences mentioned earlier, but we are also emotionally nd temperamentally different, too. God gave us feelings and motions, as well as gifts and abilities. And to each one of us las been given a distinctive personality which, contrary to ome Christian teaching, should not be negated. God uses us vithin the context of our gifts and personalities. What would ave happened in the early Church if Peter had refused to ccept the role of leadership on the grounds that, being a

rather impetuous and up-front person he must deny himsel
and skulk in the background? Certainly there were man
traits in his personality that the Lord corrected. When Jesu
first met Simon Peter He saw in him the unstable sanguin
who would defend Him one moment and deny Him the next
He saw the Peter who would break the awesome silenc
following the Transfiguration, a silence he could not stand
by suggesting that three booths should be made, one fo
Jesus, one for Moses and one for Elijah. He received a rebuk
from heaven for that! It was the same Peter who was able t
rise to a greater height of belief and insight than the othe
disciples, 'Thou art the Christ, the Son of the living God'
(Matt. 16:16AV), who later sank to the depths, even rebukin
the Lord for His mention of His coming death. That calle
forth from Jesus, 'Get thee behind me Satan', (Mar
8:33AV). At that first meeting Jesus recognised him a
unstable Simon, yet saw in him Peter the rock with stable
leadership material. God never changed his temperament o
personality, but moulded it to become Christlike, yet sti
Peter.

Later Peter was to hand over the leadership of the Churc
to the practical administrator, James, because those qualitie
were needed in the Church at that time.

Paul was of a different temperament. He was more of
driving, forceful personality, a man of one aim. He would no
have had time for the vacillating behaviour of Peter as we se
in the confrontation that took place in Antioch. In Galatian
2 we read that Peter had happily eaten with the Gentiles unt
the orthodox Jewish leaders appeared. Then Peter, true to hi
temperament, got scared and withdrew from this fellowship
Not so Paul. He would not do such a thing – the fear of ma
was not one of his problems – and he roundly chastised Pete
for his cowardice. Tradition has it that Peter was crucifie
like his Lord – no coward there.

The Church needed Paul and Peter and the gentl

encouraging Barnabas. All totally different, but each with a vital contribution to make.

The Apostle John was more the meditative type of temperament with a rather negative, paranoid tendency of the melancholic. When going with Jesus through the towns of Samaria, because the Samaritans thought Jesus and His disciples were only passing through they failed to welcome them. This brought forth great anger from John and his brother, James. Jesus told them that they did not know what type of spirit was in them, a spirit that needed tempering. At that time John was known as one of the sons of thunder – later he was known as the apostle of love. The same temperament that was easily affronted and quick to revenge when moulded by the Lord was, because of its very sensitivity, able to show the love for the Lord and for his fellow-believers that is exemplified in both the Gospel and the Epistles of John. How fitting that to the contemplative John was given the glorious revelation of God's glory and the consummation of the age.

When I was a student at Bible college we spent one term studying temperaments, and not only did I find it a fascinating study but also a liberating one. I began to understand and know myself better. Some things I had been troubled about and had looked upon as spiritual malaise; now I realised they were part of my temperament, and although my temperament wouldn't change, these weaknesses in it could and should be changed. That made a great difference in my life. It also helped me to understand my fellow-students, especially one with whom I had a hard time getting along. She irritated me and rubbed me up the wrong way constantly. You can imagine my feelings when one term she and I were assigned to work together on several projects. I wondered if the staff knew! She and I had totally different temperaments and I am sure that I was as irritating to her as she was to me. It was good to study her temperament, picking out the good points and realising that her weak points though different from mine were no worse. I did eventually learn to get on with her, even learning to appreciate her.

Although God has given us our temperaments, I do believe He wants to work on the weaknesses, as He did with the disciples. Never should we say, 'This is my temperament. I can't help losing my temper because that's the way I am.' Yes, you can do something about your temper, or your moods. (The Lord is as able to change you from a son or daughter of thunder to a person of love and patience as He was able to change James and John.) But it is helpful to know what temperament you have, with its strengths and weaknesses, and so without over simplifying it, here is a theory that has been used by many, even some leading psychiatrists. This theory deals with four basic categories of temperament: sanguine, melancholic, choleric and phlegmatic.

SANGUINE – THE ENJOYMENT TEMPERAMENT

Sanguines live in and enjoy the present. They do not brood deeply over impressions gained, but are anxious to gain as many impressions as possible. They are light-hearted people and therefore a pleasure to have around. There is never any lack of conversation when a Sanguine is present. The delight to share impressions received is always to the fore. When sorrow comes, tears may be quickly shed, but equally quickly joy will return. The Sanguine generally does not harbour slights and is quick to forgive and ask forgiveness. Because emotions in the Sanguine are uppermost, every experience is 'lived in' and communication is graphic. The Sanguine is good with children and really enters into their lives.

One of the great drawbacks of this temperament is inconstancy and this is particularly noticeable in the realm of friendship. The Sanguine is quickly interested in a thing or

person and gives it full attention – but for a time only.
Another more interesting thing or person comes along and
attention is immediately given to them. Thus we see a rather
unreliable person. However, because of initiative and
enthusiasm there is ability to gather others around and
assume leadership. There is openness of character with
feelings seldom hidden. Often, in good-heartedness, promises
will be made with full intention of their being kept, but
because other thoughts and impressions will have come along
in the meantime, the promises will have been forgotten. There
is a great capacity for living and sympathising and these
qualities can be of great usefulness if discipline is applied in
the weak areas.

Faithfulness would be another area to be worked at and
consistency in the Christian life. Excessive love of activity
could easily take the place of devotional practices. On the
other hand the delightful manner and ease of communication
would be a great aid in witnessing and helping others. Offence
would seldom be taken by an unbeliever at the winsomeness
of a Sanguine's witness.

The weak points in any temperament are due to the
presence of sin in us which gives us a natural bias to evil
(Rom. 3:12), but although it is true that our particular
temperament (or more accurately) our particular combin-
ation of the temperaments) follows us from the cradle to the
grave, the weaknesses need not. As Christ died to save us
from the penalty of sin, He also died to save us from the
power of sin, and to change these weaknesses in our
temperaments. At the beginning of this chapter, I outlined
how He worked in the life of Peter, a real Sanguine, and made
him rocklike and dependable.

MELANCHOLIC – THE SUFFERING TEMPERAMENT

Unlike the Sanguines, Melancholics tend to live in the past.

They do not retain as many impressions as the Sanguines because they weigh up all impressions, deciding what they want to keep and discarding the rest. The impressions they keep are usually on the darker, more negative side. They are deep thinkers, and this temperament has given the world many musicians, poets, artists and philosophers. Melancholics suffer deeply because of their temperament – they might also be said to delight in grief! They are suspicious of things said and easily take offence. Unlike Sanguines, they are not so easy to have around because of their somewhat pessimistic attitude to life. On the other hand, a great point in their favour is their dependability and faithfulness in interests and friends. They make few friends and have few interests, but those which they have they stick with fervently. Unlike Sanguines, they faithfully remember both duties and promises. If a promise should be broken it would no doubt be remembered and grieved over as long as life would last. Socially, Melancholics are shy, awkward and very reserved. They have difficulty in expressing themselves so tend to 'bottle things up'. They are very courteous and meticulous in affairs and in dress. Tidiness and orderliness are strong characteristics of this temperament. It has been said that the marked difference between a Sanguine and a Melancholic would be seen in the way each would pack a suitcase!

Because Melancholics tend to live in a world of thought, mostly centring on themselves, they are not normally very practical and lack initiative. Unlike Sanguines, they are not, as a rule, quick to see what should be done and get on with it. On the other hand, when it comes to making decisions they carefully weigh up all the circumstances before deciding. They are idealistic and critical in relation to others. No one quite measures up to the standard of a Melancholic, hence few friendships are cultivated. Because of the suffering temperament, a life of sacrifice and difficulty readily appeals, though a vocation or job could be dropped if it proved to be too humdrum.

CHOLERIC – THE DRIVING TEMPERAMENT

The characteristics of this temperament are a strong will, keen intellect, much initiative and ability to lead others. This can become a domineering of others in the desire for their own way and the ideas they feel are best. Cholerics feel passionately about things and thus when given a good cause they are most valuable members of society. Because of their strong-willed personality and ability they tend to become harsh, usually having little sympathy with the faults and problems of others. Their pride sometimes leads them into deception and hypocrisy to cover up their own failures. Once hurt they can become bitter and taken to the furthest extreme can become cruel. Friendships are real but undemonstrative in affection.

Converted Cholerics have great potential for Christian leadership and godliness of life. They are willing to bear hardship and sacrifice, to discipline themselves, and because of their strong will are more able than most to banish distraction of the mind which hinders prayer and meditation. They are diligent and active in their work, seldom discouraged and born organisers. Where they are engaged in teaching, the air of authority and ability to impart knowledge with few words coupled with their natural enthusiasm are of great value.

PHLEGMATIC – THE TEMPERAMENT OF EASE AND COMFORT

Phlegmatics are never greatly disturbed by impressions of any sort, and usually seek the line of least resistance. They are generally rather slow, not easily inclined to work, but when they do get to it, prove themselves persevering. They are not upset by slights from others and are not easily alarmed. They need to guard most carefully against their love of ease and eating and drinking. Like Sanguines, they would do well to take Paul's example to heart and keep their bodies in subjection (1 Cor. 9:27AV). Converted Phlegmatics can with the help of the Holy Spirit, develop rocklike stability because of their inability to get excited over things. Phlegmatics are usually the calming influence in a group and so make invaluable team members. They are able to make good decisions because they weigh things up calmly. Once their tendency to slothfulness is taken in hand they are good at persevering in routine work. Although they may never make leaders they are good, faithful followers.

Have you decided where you fit into this? We all have something of all four characteristics in us so you will have doubtless identified something of yourself in each temperament. However, we have two that predominate and it is helpful to identify these, looking at both the strong and weak points. The weak points we should ask the Lord to help us overcome, but knowing that they are part of our temperament can keep us from feeling over-guilty and will enable us to deal with them in the right way. Christ had the perfect balance of all four temperaments in Him. As He took the Sanguine Peter and made him rocklike and stable; or the Melancholic John and turned him into the apostle of love; or later He worked in the heart of Choleric Paul, who was breathing out threatenings and slaughter towards the early Church, and made him a man who would tend and nurture the same Church. So Christ can transform your temperament. Accepting the way God made you, emotionally, and co-operating with Him to perfect and channel your strengths and deal with your weaknesses, are other ingredients in a true sense of self-worth.

WE ARE FEARFULLY AND WONDERFULLY MADE – SPIRITUALLY

Not only did God make us physical and emotional beings with the capacity to love, to see and enjoy beauty, and to have relationships with other humans, He also created us to know and love Him. When sin entered the world our relationship with God was spoiled and the Bible tells us that in our natural state we are 'dead in... sins' (Eph. 2:1), cut off from fellowship with God. No wonder we are prey to frustrations and emptiness. We are failing to achieve the very purpose for which we were created. If we are to live fulfilled lives as singles we need first to experience the spiritual fulfilment of knowing God. 'Now this is eternal life: that they may know you, the only true God, and Jesus Christ, whom you have sent' (John 17:3). We can never be complete as persons if we do not know God, because the greatest dimension of our personality has been missed out. The philosopher, Pascal, said 'In the heart of every man is a God-shaped vacuum that only God can fill.' I would go further and say that at the heart of every activity – everything, everyone and indeed the universe itself – there lurks a void which only God can adequately and satisfactorily fill. Many people put down their feeling of 'lostness' to a missing ingredient – in the shape of people or activities or things. Singles may think this missing ingredient is a life partner and that marriage would make all the difference. Sometimes they get married to the 'right person' only to find that the 'lostness' and incompleteness are still there. Then they blame the partner.

Many a marriage has come unstuck because of such wrong expectations. We should never look to another person to do for us what only God can do. Christ came to earth to bring us abundant life (John 10:10) – to touch every area of our life through renewing the relationship with God for which we were created. Christ died not only to restore the relationship with God but also to enable us to become the people God

intended us to be. We all know that Romans 8:28 tell us that
for the children of God all things work together for good,
even though it may not seem like it at the time. Yet I wonder
how many of us go on to read the next verse (29) which tells us
that the purpose of our calling (to know God) was to make us
like His Son, Jesus Christ. When we talk about self-worth, I
am not referring to the sinful fleshly part of us that has no
good in it as Paul reminds us (Rom. 7:18). That is why I have
subtitled this chapter, 'The Biblical concept of self-worth'. I
believe the Bible teaches that we were created in the image of
God. When sin entered, that image was somewhat marred,
but not entirely destroyed. Christ died to bring us back to
God, and by His Spirit in us to remake that godly image. As a
Christian I am known by God fully, as we see in Psalm 139,
and yet fully accepted. How wonderful to know that
somebody knows me, warts and all, and yet still loves me!

FEELINGS OF GUILT

One of the great hindrances to a sense of Biblical self-worth is
the carrying of a burden of guilt. When we sin we must
sincerely ask the Lord for forgiveness and we shall be
forgiven. 'If we confess our sins, he is faithful and just to
forgive us our sins, and to cleanse us from all unrighteous-
ness' (1 John 1:9AV).

Often I have heard people say, 'I know I am forgiven by
God, but I cannot forgive myself'. This is not only un-
scriptural, it is also very damaging to the person. It may seem
hard, and paradoxical to say this, but pride really lies at the
root of this problem. When I say, 'I cannot forgive myself', I
am refusing to accept God's forgiveness fully, choosing rather
to inflict punishment on myself which can never atone for the
sin. The perfect atonement has already been made by Christ'
death. I always like the illustration of Corrie ten Boom who
said that God has cast all our sins into the depths of the sea

(Mic. 7:19) and He's put up a sign saying 'No fishing'. For anyone seriously burdened with this problem may I commend to your study the following verses: Isaiah 38:17; 43:25; Psalm 103:12, and 1 John 1:9. Look these verses up in the Bible, meditate on them, commit them to memory, pray over them and claim them for your own. Then count on them knowing that 'God had power to do what he had promised' for *you* (Rom. 4:21).

Accepting the way God made you, spiritually, and co-operating with His laws and His work in your life is another – and very vital – ingredient in a sense of true self-worth.

So, to build a true sense of our own worth we must accept and apply these basic facts.

OVERCOMING THE PAST

But what about those early experiences I mentioned before? If they have been destructive, will they not continue to hamper us for the rest of our lives? I believe not. I believe that we can do something about our attitudes and that God will meet us when we do and will transform us and therefore the effect of that situation or experience on us.

I knew a young woman who had come from a terrible background. Both her parents were alcoholics and to quote her own words she was 'dragged up'. This left some terrible scars on her personality and sometimes she would despair of ever 'making it'. Then she accepted Christ and it made a difference in her life. After some time, she came to the Bible College at which I was teaching. While there, the traumatic upbringing she had had was very obvious and some of us on the staff almost despaired of her. But at the beginning of her second year she came back transformed.

What had happened? Everybody was agog to know. She told us that at the end of the previous term, one day in utter despair, she had got down on her knees by her bed with her open Bible and prayed something like this: 'Lord you know all about my life, my upbringing, my parents and all the mess that this has produced in my life. Now Lord, if you are the God you say you are in your Word, able to perform miracles for the blind, the leper, and even raise the dead, you are able to help me. I am not going to allow all that's happened in the past to spoil my life for the future so, Lord, I hand over to you my bitterness, and my weakness and all that I am to you. Make me the person you want me to be.' And God took her at her word and we saw a changed young woman. If God can do that for her He can do that for you and for me if we are willing.

Some singles feel that they are second-class citizens and that being single damages their self-image. This is not true, but if you think like that it may become true for you. Later we shall discuss how the attitude of the world can give rise to this but for now let us think of our own attitudes.

DEALING WITH THE HURT

If there is bitterness over the past it must be dealt with. As we thought in the previous chapter, bitterness is like a spiritual infection and until there is a rooting out healing cannot take place. What can you do about it?

1. You must recognise the bitterness and confess it, asking for forgiveness.
2. Then thank the Lord for your parents, background, singleness, whatever it is. After all, your parents gave you life so there is that to thank them for, and often when we think hard enough we find something to appreciate in a person, or even an adverse situation. Think of something good in your background, maybe a very small thing. Even the fact that you are single, if you resent this at the moment, means you are not stuck in an unhappy marriage; you are

free to come and go as you please. This thankfulness is an act of the will, not emotions.

3. Promise to co-operate with God in the future in developing the character qualities that He desires. Remember, as with the Bible College student, God wants to bring the best out of a situation, even one that seems so bad to us.

4. Avoid comparing yourself with others (2 Cor. 10:12). God has made you unique, given you gifts, and wants to use you.

How, then, do we start building a true sense of our own worth? Briefly – we encourage ourselves, perhaps daily, in the fact that God made us and loves us as we are, recognising that the only changes He wants to make are those that are necessary if we are to become the people we were designed to be and will therefore be at our happiest and best in so being; we should also deal with our attitude before God in relation to negative experiences.

BE AN ENCOURAGER

And having encouraged ourselves in God – let's encourage others.

I have a friend, a woman of few words, from whom, whenever I am around her, I sense encouragement and the feeling that she believes in me. She always makes me feel good and consequently brings out the best in me.

I once heard a speaker begin a meeting by saying, 'I want to talk about the Church's most neglected ministry.' My mind raced ahead to many subjects he might cover. Imagine my surprise when he said, 'The ministry of encouragement.' But how right he was. Encouragement is a grossly neglected ministry. Sometimes we think that to encourage someone for work well done, or just to show appreciation for the person

will produce pride. How misguided we are. Men and women
can become intensely proud, constantly drawing attention to
themselves and their abilities because they are not receiving
encouragement and recognition. But if they felt they were
appreciated and heard *words* of appreciation, they would not
feel the need to push themselves forward for survival. Many
singles who live alone seldom hear words of encouragement
about appearance or performance. Why not make that your
ministry, to be an ENCOURAGER?

Somebody once wrote a book on encouragement entitled.
Don't wait till he's dead. What eulogies we give people at their
funerals. They would probably be amazed to know how
people thought about them because there was no such
indication in their lifetime. Let us seek to enrich others' lives
now by encouragement and appreciation. Let us be specific in
saying *what* we appreciate about the other person. This is
more helpful than vague generalities, and more likely to be
believed, too! Everybody works better with encouragement
and perhaps this is borne out by the Scriptural injunction.
'And let us consider how we may spur one another on
towards love and good deeds' (Heb. 10:24).

A man with a good and accurate assessment of himself
said: 'I am fearfully and wonderfully made: marvellous are
thy works; and that *my soul knoweth right well*' (Ps. 139
14AV). David knew that he was a person of worth, not just in
his mind but in his soul – deep down inside. He was a man
with a good self-image. Yet he was a man whose self-image
could have been shattered and his sense of significance and
security – essential to us all – could have been destroyed
Destroyed by his own sin: he not only committed adultery but
also murder to cover his traces (2 Sam. 11): destroyed by
bitterness over his ill-treatment by Saul or the scorn of his
wife, Michal, when she despised him for dancing before the
Lord (2 Sam. 6:20); or by the terrible disloyalty of his much-
loved son Absalom (2 Sam. 15). But he didn't allow that to
happen. He received God's forgiveness and dealt firmly with

his own attitudes. He encouraged himself in God and became an encourager of others.

We are so like him in our human frailty aren't we? Let's follow his example in these other ways and gain a true sense of self-worth.

In the next chapter we shall consider some specific ways that singles can have a vital ministry.

3

BEING AN ATTRACTIVE SINGLE
(How do you come across?)

During a singles conference attended by a friend of mine someone suggested what seemed to be a worthwhile exercise: think of the most attractive single whom you know. List the qualities that you consider go to make up that person's attractiveness.

When I think of an attractive single, I think of at least three areas of attractiveness: personality traits, appearance and environment.

ATTRACTIVE PERSONALITY TRAITS

As I was thinking about the exercise suggested at the conference, I remembered a woman I had known some years before and about whom I had thought, If I reach her age (she was probably in her mid-fifties at the time) and I am as happy, fulfilled and balanced as she is, I shan't mind being single.

Since meeting this woman, I have met many other single women with attractive personality traits. They haven't conformed at all to the 'frustrated spinster' image. Instead, they have obviously enjoyed their work and their social life and contributed greatly to the circle of people among whom they have moved. The same could be said of many single men.

Such people can be a powerful testimony to the satisfying power of Christ.

I will say more later about attractive personality traits, but first I should like to identify some unattractive ones.

UNATTRACTIVE PERSONALITY TRAITS

Not all singles are like the people I referred to above. Some have very off-putting characteristics. Before enlarging on some of these, let me hasten to add that what follows could apply to married people – some of whom appear to have married in spite rather than because of their personalities!

Abrasiveness

'You'll like Jane, when you get to know her.' 'John's a really nice fellow. It's just his rather brusque manner that puts people off at first.' How often have we heard remarks like these!

A few years ago I was asked to help a young single Christian who was being given a hard time by the other girls in the hostel where she lived, because (according to her) she was a Christian. Immediately I heard that, a red light came on in my mind, but I decided to reserve my judgment until after I had met her. A few days later she arrived on my doorstep. I soon understood the feelings of the people she lived with, and why they had reacted so negatively towards her. My first impression was of an unsmiling stare, and an abrupt, abrasive personality which, later on, I found hard to penetrate. I was a Christian wanting to befriend this girl, but it took a lot of time, energy and prayer before I came to know her. It took even longer, with more prayer and love, to see her finally melt and become a warmer and more loving personality. It wasn't because she was a Christian that she was disliked. It was because she had a very abrasive personality which put people off. But, as she came to realise, it was a problem she could do something about.

What do I mean by an abrasive personality? If a material is abrasive and you knock against it, you will get bruised or skinned and this will hurt. If you knock against something soft and pliable you won't get hurt; perhaps you'll even be cushioned by it. We can apply this to relationships. Some people come over as sharp and critical and we feel they would give us a hard time if we were to put a foot wrong. They pride themselves on 'speaking the truth', 'being honest', 'telling it like it is', but in so doing they appear harsh and critical. They seem to forget that we are told to speak 'the truth *in love*' (Eph. 4:15 my italics). It is good to be open and honest with one another, but it must be done with a motive of love and in a loving way. We need first to win the right to tell someone a home-truth by gaining that person's friendship and confidence. Much damage has been done in churches where people have taken it upon themselves to 'put people right'.

I know some Christians with whom I would never share my failures and ask for prayer because I sense they would be very critical, perhaps shocked, and would undoubtedly deliver a sermon! This doesn't mean that I would only turn to people who sympathise and agree with me. But it does mean that I turn to those who are capable of making constructive, objective comments while being empathetic and understanding.

Sometimes abrasiveness can show itself in the form of jokes at others' expense. I had a friend who often used to come over for dinner when I was sharing a flat some years ago. We always enjoyed her company because she was good fun and we always knew we would have some good laughs when she came. But after a while we realised that the jokes that she made and at which we laughed so uproariously were jokes at others' expense. When we came to realise this, the amusement went out of the jokes for us. Jokes at others' expense, or comments belittling others, are unworthy of

Christians and cause hurt to those on the receiving end. On the other hand, helping each other in a spirit of love benefits both parties.

Sometimes we think that aggressiveness is a sign of strength. Often this is not so. Aggression can be a cover-up for deep insecurities. The person who is gentle and able to control his temper is probably the really strong one. Moses, who led the children of Israel through the wilderness for forty years and put up with all their grumblings and was often provoked to anger by their behaviour, is described as 'a very humble man, more humble than anyone else on the face of the earth' (Num. 12:3). Yet what a strong man he must have been to have led God's people at that great time in their history. Gentleness and meekness are qualities of strength not weakness.

'As a company of the forgiven, we are the most unforgiving people'. So said a conference speaker and I believe he was saying something very true, albeit very sad. How harshly we condemn a fellow-Christian who offends, forgetting how easily we could do the same thing. Or we self-righteously think we would never do that and fail to see the other things we do which are equally offensive to others.

'Every time he opens his mouth he puts his foot in it.' 'I always manage to say the wrong things.' You have probably often heard these expressions, or said them about yourself. What can we do if we are like that? Or worse still, what if we do these things *without realising it*? Your friends will realise it even if you don't. So if you have a close and trusted friend in whom you can confide, ask him or her to tell you how you come over to others – and when you 'put your foot in it', If you don't have anyone like that, ask the Lord to show you if these characteristics are true of you. He will certainly do this and help you to deal with the problem. One of the most wonderful things about the conviction of the Holy Spirit is that He never leaves you feeling hopeless and helpless. When He *convicts* there is always a feeling of hope and usually the sense of what can be done – if not immediately, then certainly after more prayer.

Mousiness

Having thought about the abrasive or aggressive person it would also be important to stress that God does not want us to be non-persons either. God has given each of us a distinct personality which He wants us to develop and use to His glory. He has also given us the ability to make decisions and choices of our own and it is important to our psychological well-being that we use this ability.

Keep yourself interesting. Know what is going on in the world and be able to converse intelligently. It bothers me a great deal when Christians rather sanctimoniously say they never watch TV or read the newspapers, because they haven't time, or some other such reason. There is a great need today for Christians to be well-informed and ready to give an opinion – we should not be known as the silent minority because we are uninformed. Certainly we should be very discerning over our TV viewing, and be prepared to speak out when something is offensive, but there is much we can and should know about our world that will keep us from being insular and self-absorbed. How would the world know about the disasters and famines that take place in other parts if it weren't for excellent TV coverage?

Be a positive person. Christians should never be satisfied merely with avoiding evil or indeed any other aspect of reality. They should go out as God's agents, working positively for the spread of righteousness and every other positive godly quality in the world. God does not want mice. He wants men and women growing more like Jesus, becoming strong and confident in His strength.

Perhaps it would be good to say something here about the way we express our views. It is important that we show ourselves as people with an opinion but not opinionated. And we shouldn't necessarily expect that what we say will always be implemented. A good boss should always welcome the opinions and views of those he works with, although he is not bound to act on them. Being like 'a bull in a china shop' will almost always produce a negative reaction and even good advice could be dismissed because of the way it is given. Much more attention is paid to what is said by the person who remains cool in a situation and can quietly and rationally 'state their case', than to what is said in a heated, emotional way.

Some years ago I was in a work situation which often made me rather upset over what I felt were injustices and dishonesties. At staff meetings I would get very uptight, and sometimes quite indignant. This would be noticed in the way I spoke – my voice would get higher in pitch and volume. One day a colleague cautioned me about this, explaining that by being continually like dynamite that never goes off I was losing my effectiveness. She suggested that if I stated what I had to say in a calmer way it would be far more readily received. I followed her advice and found she was right.

I am not suggesting anger is always wrong. Much depends on the motive behind it and the way it is expressed. *Uncontrolled* anger is always wrong and need never be the experience of the Christian. The Lord died to save us, not just from the penalty of sin, but also from its power, so we can hand over anger to the controlling power of the Holy Spirit.

Moodiness

What about the person who is moody? This is not only difficult for the moody person but also for those around them. We are all subject to moods and these can be affected by circumstances, hormones, time of the month and heredity, but we need not be mastered by our moods. Our temperaments are relevant here, but we should not excuse our moodiness by saying 'That's the way I am, I can't help it.'

Moodiness can and should be controlled. I remember when I was in nursing training one of the ward sisters under whom I worked allowed herself to be dominated by her moods. We came to dread Monday mornings after her weekends off because she would always be in a foul mood, slamming the door of her office. Woe betide anyone who crossed her! The staff were aware of this and so – which was even worse – were the patients. It was a very unhappy and damaging situation for all concerned. For the Christian such behaviour is inexcusable. The Lord who gave us our temperaments is also able to control our moods, and we should ask Him to do so.

This does not mean that we should not be alive to our feelings. On the contrary, it is *unacknowledged* emotions that do us harm. We must acknowledge our emotions and then decide whether it would be helpful to express them or not. Some Christians act as though it were a sin to express anything other than a smile and sometimes the smile looks as though it had frozen on their lips!

Be honest with yourself and God as to how you feel. If you have a hard time coming alive in the morning there's nothing wrong in admitting that. But it would be good to ask the Lord to help you to wake up with a sense of joy, looking forward to a new day. For many years I woke up slightly depressed and not particularly looking forward to the day ahead. That made it very hard for me to get out of bed. When my early-morning quiet time became important to me, things started to change for me in this respect. A friend of mine considered herself a night-owl and went to bed very late, sometimes preferring to study until the early hours of the morning before falling into bed, only to rise late and rush to work. One day she discovered the joy of rising early to meet with the Lord for prayer and Bible study, and her whole life changed. When I knew her, her daily habit was to rise at 5 a.m. for two hours of prayer and study. She was a woman whom God greatly used.

For women, premenstrual tension can cause mood swings.

This can certainly be helped by praying and planning ahead
to counteract this. If severe symptoms appear it is good to
consult a doctor as steps can be taken to alleviate these. But
often it is a case of accepting the situation, not fighting
against it, and praying about it as well as planning your time
sensibly, taking account of your physical and mental state.
Physical conditions can certainly affect mood. High blood
pressure, illness, the menopause for women, the mid-life
crisis for men, are just some of the conditions that can cause
depression or mood variations. Don't try and be hyper-
spiritual about it. Accept it as a fact of life and consult your
doctor. If pills are prescribed to see you over a period of time
don't feel that it's necessarily wrong to take them. God works
through these means, too. But having sought medical advice,
and been given treatment, then the situation needs to be
faced, accepted and lived through. Ultimately it is a matter of
choice. I choose whether or not I will allow my moodiness to
dominate and affect others or whether I will keep it under
control, and as a Christian I should want to be attractive – in
mood, as in other ways, including appearance.

An attractive appearance

'Man looks on the outward appearance, but the Lord looks at
the heart' (1 Sam. 16:7). How often we emphasise the second
part of the verse and forget that the first part is equally true.
Man does look at the outward appearance and it is a very true
saying that first impressions are important. Christians have
often been recognised by their dowdy appearance and not
only is this sad, it is also a very poor testimony to the Lord.
Jesus Himself had no money of His own – He even allowed a
fish to supply His tax money (Matt. 17:24-7) – yet we read
that when He was on the cross and the soldiers were casting
lots for His clothes they would not divide His coat but
gambled for the intact garment. So it must have been of good

appearance or quality – well worth wearing.

Fortunately, things have changed for the better in the Christian scene. People are taking more trouble over appearance. Don't misunderstand me, I'm not saying we should all dress elegantly or expensively. What I am saying is – study yourself, and find out what suits you and your lifestyle and enjoy that. If you prefer casual clothes there is nothing wrong with that. If you are a person who looks good in bright colours, don't be afraid to wear them. I met a girl at a meeting not so long ago who was wearing a bright red cardigan. When I commented on how good she looked in the colour she replied, 'I was told that Christians shouldn't wear bright colours.'

When I returned to England after several years in California I had misgivings about some of my clothes knowing the more conservative British Christian view about dress. I am a person who can wear bright colours and enjoys wearing them. One of my favourite outfits was a bright red suit which I wore with a black blouse. I had often worn this outfit for speaking engagements while in the States as I have found that a bright colour is more likely to keep an audience alert! One particular day soon after I had arrived back in England I was booked to speak at an evangelistic home meeting. I really wrestled over whether or not I should wear my red suit. Would I shock people, and cause offence to the Christians? In the end I decided to wear it. You can imagine my relief and joy when, at the end of the meeting, a non-Christian lady (and after all I was not there to minister to Christians) said, 'I always thought Christians were drab and badly dressed until I met you and Max (a colleague of mine). Thank you for wearing that red suit.' I am not saying that everyone should wear bright colours. That would be foolish. Certain skin colours can only tolerate pastel shades and look terrible with bright colours. What I *am* saying is that as Christians we should look upon our appearance as part of our testimony and avoid the misguided view that it is spiritual to look scruffy and unkempt or to wear clothes that make us look as unattractive as possible! Everything I have said applies to men as well as women.

Taking time, perhaps with a friend who has a good eye for clothes and especially for what would suit you, to decide on some basic colours and styles, could save you much time, trouble and money and help you to feel good about yourself, whatever style you choose. If you are needing to buy an outfit, why not choose the most attractive one within your price range?

An attractive environment

Our home is an extension of our personality and should be a place we enjoy being in. Even if home is one room, already furnished, we can still make it our own. When I lived for three years in various nurses' homes with their characteristic small bedrooms already furnished with utilitarian and somewhat unaesthetic furniture, it was quite a challenge to make them feel like home to me. But with pictures, maybe a cushion or two, trinkets of various sorts, a plant – one nurse had a goldfish she lovingly tended, which barely escaped extinction when I had to look after it during her holiday – it was amazing how each room became totally different and spoke of the personality of the occupant. Some singles live at home with parents and again the place is not their own. But what they do with their bedrooms can make them feel it is theirs: a place where they can relax and be themselves. Those of you who have your own home, either rented or owned – make it a place you enjoy coming home to and spending time in. I am not talking about spending a lot of money or advocating a particular style: styles will and should vary from person to person. But a home that you enjoy can do much to relieve loneliness and depression. It is psychologically important for you to have around you in your place things that please your eye. I am concerned when I hear singles say that they never spend much time at home, only using it as a place to sleep. A single can feel at least as secure and happy in his or her own home as a married couple can in theirs.

I have had several homes, mostly rented, and I know quite a bit about second-hand furniture or doing without things until the money comes in. But in each case for me homemaking has been a fascinating and rewarding experience. When I was living and working in the States over a period of nine years I managed to acquire some lovely furniture which I moved with me when I left California and went up the West Coast to Washington for a year before coming back to England. Then I had, sadly, to sell most of my furniture because shipping it would have been well beyond my means. I kept only a few precious things: pictures, a lovely mirror, an upholstered rocking-chair, a nest of tables and, of course, masses of books. So on returning to England, I had to start virtually all over again.

My first home on arrival back in England was a furnished bed-sitting room in the home of some friends. Then, when they left to go abroad, I had to move. I was urged by concerned friends to buy my own home – something I had never thought possible after years of being on a Christian worker's salary! But this became a reality. It meant starting again, gathering furniture bit by bit, but it has all been worth it, to have a home to enjoy.

Not only do I enjoy my home, but I hope others do, too. Entertaining and giving hospitality is very important for the single person. I enjoy living alone. After years of living with others, when I was in Bible college, doing nursing training and in Christian work, I find it enjoyable to come home after a busy day to quietness and solitude and to do what I want to do. Many single people would share this feeling; others would not. Those of us who do enjoy living alone need to be careful that we do not get selfish, and to realise that we need to be accountable for wasted hours and bad habits, such as too much time spent in front of the TV! One of the ways in which we can combat selfishness is to practise hospitality as we are told to do in Romans 12:13. As I said, I enjoy living alone, but I also enjoy the fact that I have a spare room and can invite people to stay or just to come over for tea, coffee, or dinner.

Entertaining does not need to be a big production. In fact the entertaining that means most is the sort that is relaxed and simple. If we waited until all the circumstances were right, and we were going to serve the perfect meal, most of us would never have anyone in our homes. Sadly enough, many of us don't. We think of having friends over as such a major feat that it never happens. I have spoken to many singles who had said they are seldom asked out, including a widower with a grown-up son and daughter.

Is that why there are so many lonely people around today? Family life has changed. Young people move away from home as soon as they can. As more people have to work today there is no one to care for the elderly at home, so the extended family with grandparents being included in the household is very rarely seen nowadays. Much of this has come about because of the economic climate. Single women have to go out to work today, as do many married women, instead of staying at home. This has certainly given far greater freedom to pursue a fulfilling career, which, particularly for the single woman, is essential. But all of this has left people more isolated; instead of leaving work and returning to a busy family home many return to their flat or house alone – and stay there alone. We can greatly help each other and ourselves over this if we will 'practise hospitality'.

Christians individually and the Church corporately have failed badly in this area. There are many lonely people and groups of people in our churches who have to resort to outside organisations for help or just remain lonely, because the church family, as we like to think of it, is not performing its function. How often we hear someone say they gave up attending church because no one spoke to them week in and week out. Many singles that I have spoken to confess that

Sunday is the worst day of the week. They go to church, and
they come home to a solitary Sunday lunch. The wife of an
evangelist with four children told me how she dreaded
Sunday when her husband was away. Week after week she
would be in her church longing that someone would ask her
to join them for lunch, but no one did.

Yet she had four children, you say. Yes, but she was lonely
and longed for a contemporary with whom to talk and for
whom she would enjoy cooking a 'proper' Sunday lunch
instead of the sausages and chips or hamburgers her children
enjoyed. She told me that the best time she had had in several
weeks was when a single friend had asked if she could come
and join them for lunch on the Sunday. The evangelist's wife
had been able to put on a good lunch and enjoy it in the
company of her single friend.

Another widow friend of mine said she would like to start a
Sunday club for other widowed people in the area, suggesting
that they could go to each other's homes each Sunday for a
shared lunch. Everyone would be encouraged to contribute
something so that no one person would have all the burden;
and moving from home to home each Sunday with a different
host or hostess perhaps providing the meat course each time
would not make the financial burden too hard on anyone.
Other singles could do the same type of thing.

For many who work, the thought of having someone over
to dinner can be rather daunting. Knowing my love of
entertaining, a friend gave me a slow-cooker and it has been
invaluable. A book of recipes comes with it and they are quite
simple. My cooker makes it possible for me to prepare food
(not taking too much time) before I go to work and leave it
quite happily, knowing that nothing will burn and that
because of the slow cooking, all the nutrients will be retained
in the food and the flavour will be delicious. So if you, like
me, are a rather apprehensive cook, with only a few basic
recipes, you can use this method and always be confident of a

tasty meal. Single men who like to entertain would find it invaluable, too.

Don't be afraid of entertaining couples. Some singles drop their friends when the friends marry. Our married friends need us as much as we need them and this is all part of being in the family of God. When I entertain my married friends I will often invite two couples and I make the fifth person. That means they can talk to each other when I have to be in the kitchen for a moment or two. I never try to pair myself off, and hope, when I go to the homes of my married friends, that they don't try and pair me off either. This can be very unsubtle and embarrassing for all concerned.

ATTRACTIVE PERSONALITY TRAITS: A SUMMARY

So, to return to the exercise referred to at the beginning of this chapter, I would say that the most attractive single person (or indeed married person) whom I could envisage would be someone who enjoyed life to the full; someone who knew and accepted themselves and was in control of themselves; a person who was neither aggressive nor mousy, but had the right kind of confidence that set them free to make the best of themselves and their circumstances and environment.

Such a person would increasingly realise the potential that God has for them in helping and reaching out to others.

In the next chapter we shall consider some of the special pressures that we encounter as singles and the ways we can choose to regard them.

4

STUMBLING-BLOCKS
OR STEPPING-STONES
(Problems to be faced in the single life)

It's so easy to talk about coming to terms with singleness, but not so easy to put this into practice. In this chapter I want to mention some of the pressures which single people have to face and to show that these can defeat them or help them to grow stronger and more whole.

THE PRESSURE TO MARRY

'I can't understand why an attractive girl like you is not married.' 'It's high time, young man, that you found yourself a wife.'

Most of us singles will have heard remarks like this, probably many times, directed at us or at our friends or acquaintances. The implication behind such remarks is always the same: that something is wrong with you if you are still in the single state. One married friend went a step further and suggested that there must be something wrong with me for saying I was *happy* being single!

On one occasion, when speaking to a mixed group of singles I asked them, as I often do ask such groups, what they found hardest about being single. Almost without hesitation they said, 'social pressure'. Others have said, 'pressure from parents'. It has been interesting to me to find that this has frequently been at the top of the list of problems, even before things like loneliness or coping with sexual desire. Once I was given the opportunity of speaking to a group of twenty-five couples on how they could relate better with their single friends. In preparing for this I compiled a list of thoughtless remarks that singles often have to endure. In addition to those given there were remarks such as 'If you don't marry I'll consider it [your life] has been a waste.' This was said to a woman who had spent many years in full-time Christian service! It reminded me of the disciple's comment about the alabaster box of ointment poured on Jesus's head – which showed their totally mixed-up values (Matt. 26:8).

'How many children do you have?' 'None, I'm not married.' 'Oh. I'm sorry. I'm always putting my foot in it.' An exchange like this is not uncommon and what is said implies that the single person has a problem or is to be pitied. 'I think everybody ought to be married,' is another remark sometimes heard. Worse than that was the comment of a married man, 'I think everyone who is single is outside the will of God.' He certainly didn't get this viewpoint from the Bible.

What does the Bible say? The first verse that is usually quoted comes right at the beginning of the Bible in Genesis 2:18 where we read that God said, 'It is not good for the man to be alone. I will make him a helper suitable for him.' God then paraded the animals in front of Adam and he named them all, but 'for Adam no suitable helper was found' (v.20). And so the woman was created to be a companion and helper. Up to this point Adam had been entirely alone with no other human being at all. Certainly from this the marriage partnership springs, but at the very beginning God created woman to be an intellectual equal and work partner in the great task that He had given mankind. It was this that would combat Adam's utter aloneness.

As a single woman I am not alone. In my case I still have

family members, many friends, people I work with and
church family. We need each other and not one man or
woman should live in isolation. That doesn't mean that
everyone should marry. Just think of Jesus Christ and,
according to some traditions, the apostle Paul. Although it is
possible that he was married at some time he was obviously
single (widowed, perhaps) when he wrote 1 Corinthians 7. He
points out the fact that the single man's or woman's priority is
to put first the things of God, whereas the married man or
woman must first consider his or her spouse.

After Jesus had spoken about divorce, his disciples said, 'If
this is the situation between a husband and wife, it is better
not to marry' (Matt. 19:10). Jesus's reply to that was, 'Not
everyone can accept this teaching, but only those to whom it
has been given. For some are eunuchs because they were born
that way; others were made that way by men; and others have
renounced marriage because of the kingdom of heaven. *The
one who can accept this should accept it*' (vv. 11-12 my
italics). While the Lord is telling us here that the single life is
not for all, today we make the great mistake of thinking that it
isn't for anyone.

In Kari Torjesen Malcolm's excellent book, *Women at the
Crossroads*, she says in her chapter, 'Ministering as a Single
Woman',

Sex is not the only drive within us. We also have a drive to
succeed, an urge to develop our abilities and use them for
God's glory. Middle-aged women often look back on lost
opportunities to become all that God intended them to be.
Among these women, a number have admitted that they
would have been far better off if they had remained single
and found their fulfilment in creative activity as an
alternative expression of their sexuality. Others have
confessed with tears that as teenagers they dedicated their
lives to God's service. But instead of considering marriage
only if they met a man for whom Jesus Christ also came

first, they left their first love for the love of a mere human being.

Kari Malcolm, herself a happily married woman, makes a very valid point, I believe.

Whereas it is true to say that the majority of people want to marry, and will marry, it is also true that there are those who have no desire in this direction and find great fulfilment in a career. There are also many men and women who do not especially desire children of their own and yet love children and work well with them as teachers or nurses. There is nothing wrong with these people and we are blindly accepting the world's stereotypes when we assume that there is. To the world the norm is getting married and having children – preferably two! Such social attitudes cause heartaches to singles and to childless couples.

THE PRESSURE TO HAVE SEX

Sex is a god to many today. We see it exalted on TV on newsstands, in advertising and in a hundred different ways. Sexappeal is a sought-after attribute and many feel their personal worth depends on it. But as I have already said (Chapter 2), I cannot go along with this attitude. The world's value system seems all awry – like a shop in which all the price-tags have been switched so that those of the greatest value are priced cheaply and the cheap and tawdry things are priced highly.

Morality and integrity are laughed at as 'old-fashioned' qualities while sexual promiscuity is considered smart and normal. For those who are single, sex outside of marriage or homosexuality are put forward as 'acceptable' alternative lifestyles. But for the Christian they are *not*, according to the Bible which has much to say about both. For example: 'It is God's will that you should be holy; that you should avoid sexual immorality' (1 Thess. 4:3).

God created sex to be enjoyed within the confines of th
marriage union, and the sexual union means that two person
become one flesh till death parts them. Many people toda
want to have sex before marriage, some feel marriage is no
even necessary, providing they have a partner. This is no
God's plan and therefore is not an option for the Christian. I
1 Corinthians 6:18, when Paul cautions us to 'flee from sexua
immorality', he also goes on to explain, 'All other sins a ma
commits are outside his body, but he who sins sexually sin
against his own body. Do you not know that your body is
temple of the Holy Spirit, who is in you, whom you hav
received from God? You are not your own; you were bough
at a price. Therefore honour God with your body' (v. 19,20)
The phrase 'You are not your own', revolutionised my ow
thinking as I realised that I belonged to someone for whom
had to keep myself pure in every way. The way I *think* wil
determine the way I act; and in coping with sexual desires it i
very much a matter of controlling the mind and will – abou
which I want to say more later on.

It is always hard to swim against the stream: as singles w
often feel that we are battling against the stream of publi
opinion, the normal course of life's events (i.e. being married
and our own feelings. And this can often make it very hard fo
us. Perhaps we forget that as *Christians* we are all swimmin
against the stream: we are often thought very odd an
experience a certain amount of ridicule because we hav
chosen to follow the Lord. Does that embarrass us or make u
feel ashamed? I trust not. On the contrary the committe
Christian delights to tell others about the Saviour and seek
to persuade others to follow Him.

Like normal sex outside marriage, homosexuality is als
condemned in the Bible, both in the Old and New Testament
(Leviticus 18:22 and Romans 1:26-7 to mention just tw
passages). If you are aware that this is your sexual preference
you can and should seek help. Again, this is another are
where the Christian is going against much of today's strear

of thinking, but the Bible is clear on this (1 Cor. 6:9-11). And, as you'll have noticed in the passage, not only homosexuality but all types of sexual immorality are mentioned as coming under God's judgment. Verse 11 gives the encouragement of showing that there is a way out, with full forgiveness and restoration, and the power to keep straight by the Spirit of our God.

BEING MISUNDERSTOOD

Some singles who are not homosexual and have no inclination this way are, however, labelled with this simply because they are single. This has often happened to single men, but increasingly now it is happening to single women. My advice to both sexes would be:

1. Don't become paranoid and assume that everyone thinks like this. They don't – not by a long way.
2. Avoid giving anyone occasion to think you might be homosexually inclined. Let me illustrate. I have two good friends, women, who have lived together for some time. One day, while one of them was on her knees weeding in the front garden, her friend came bounding up the front path overjoyed at some wonderful news – the answer to long and earnest prayer of both of them. Of course they were thrilled as the news was shared, and after kneeling down to share a hug they overbalanced and with much laughter landed up in a heap on the grass. Imagine their shock and dismay a few days later when an anonymous letter arrived from one of the neighbours who had observed the incident. It stated in no uncertain terms that what they had seen 'proved' what they had already suspected! It is sad that even innocent enjoyment of good news can occasion evil thoughts and actions. But that is the world in which we live and Paul's words are as applicable

now as they were when he wrote to the young Thessalonian
Church, 'Abstain from all appearance of evil' (1 Thess.
5:22AV).
3. If asked a direct question, give a direct answer. Perhaps
your answer should make it clear that you have no
homosexual leanings and convey your stand (with
Scriptural backing) in the matter.

THE PRESSURE OF LONELINESS

As a sociologist once said, 'Loneliness is a form of distress
more common than the common cold, and infinitely more
upsetting, yet we do not talk about it.'

You would scarcely be human if you had never
experienced being lonely, so don't be afraid to admit it and
let's talk about it now.

What is loneliness? It certainly isn't just solitude because
we all need that. In fact, having space and privacy is very
important to human beings and great tensions can build up if
these are absent. Audrey Wetherall Johnson, founder of the
Bible Study Fellowship, tells about her release from a
Japanese concentration camp at the end of the Second World
War. After three years of living surrounded by 89 women and
with beds 2-3 feet apart, she found herself on her first
morning of freedom, weeping with gratitude and relief by a
beautiful river-bank. At long last she was – Oh! bliss –
completely alone. Being herded together had been one of the
hardest things to bear in those terrible years.

Sometimes we feel lonely not just among strangers but
even in the midst of our own family, where, for example, we
feel we are not really appreciated or understood. Sociologists
speak of loneliness as the need to be augmented in conditions
of stress or threat or as the feeling of not having one's
essential qualities recognised. Some singles feel lonely
because they do not have one particular person to love them

and make them feel special: 'I'm not special to anyone,' said a young woman to me at a conference. Men often feel the same way, 'Who would care if I died?' one said to me.

Loneliness is often compounded by other feelings of unhappiness. People with a low self-image through rejection in childhood are often gripped in the isolation of thinking they can never be loved by anybody, and can experience a very acute sense of loneliness even though they might be surrounded by caring people. Having a problem to discuss and no one immediately present or available to discuss it with, can greatly accentuate the fact that we are alone, that we have to cope alone, make all our own decisions.

The widowed and divorced often find this loneliness much harder to bear because they have not always been on their own. They have experienced companionship and now they are alone.

RESPONDING TO THESE PRESSURES

How can we respond to these (and other) pressures? It would be very easy to respond with self-pity and self-absorption. I am grateful to the friend who helped me not to respond in that way after a heartbreaking experience. When I'd told this friend about my experience, she surprised (and, at the time, annoyed) me by asking, 'To whom are you ministering these days?' I thought, 'How can she be so callous? I need someone to minister to me. I'm all broken up inside. I could never minister to anyone right now.' I said something of the sort to her.

In reply she read a verse to me from her Bible. '. . . if you spend yourselves on behalf of the hungry and satisfy the needs of the oppressed, then your light will rise in the darkness, and your night will become like the noonday' (Isa. 58:10).

GIVING OURSELVES TO OTHERS

The principle she was pointing out to me was that as we give ourselves to others and look to their needs and seek to help them, the very doing of it, first, takes our mind off ourselves, and then we experience the truth of this Scriptural promise that the light and blessing that comes from us as we so act will disperse the darkness that surrounds us so that the dark night that we are experiencing will give way to the brightness of noon.

I have proved this principle many times since then. Often we have heard people say following a bereavement or some other tragedy that they lost themselves in their work. As Christians, rather than losing ourselves in any work just for the sake of working, we can ask the Lord to give us a ministry to some person or persons to encourage, build up and take them on with the Lord at least as far as we've gone ourselves. Even some of the heartbreaking experiences we have been through can be used to help others through similar experiences. I admit that sometimes while counselling or discipling somebody at that heartbreaking time I just mentioned, I found myself thinking, 'I wonder if they know that my heart is breaking?' Of course they didn't and the particular experience was too new and the wound too raw, to share, but the principle worked and healing came, quicker and more effectively (I think) as a result.

EATING PROPERLY

Another common response to feeling low and lonely is to stop looking after oneself physically. In fact, it can sometimes be the other way round: we feel low simply (or largely) because we are not eating properly!

One Sunday evening my phone rang and on the other end was a distressed young woman asking if she could come round and see me. She arrived and told me in words and looks that she had been crying all day because she was so desperately lonely. Oh yes, she had been to church, but sadly that had not really helped as she had left the church without anyone speaking to her and had gone home to her bed-sit to be alone. I listened and then I asked her a question I wouldn't normally have thought to ask, but it seemed to come strongly to my mind so I put it to her. 'What have you eaten today?'

'Nothing much,' she replied. No wonder she was feeling depressed! Her low blood sugar and the general sense of fatigue that usually accompanies lack of food would both have contributed to this feeling. I explained this to her and urged her to plan a menu and eat a balanced diet. She agreed to take action on this and it was remarkable to see the difference this made to her.

It is very important to eat regularly and to have a balanced diet. Even though you may eat mostly alone, make it an occasion. Cook fresh vegetables and a meat or fish dish, if you are not a vegetarian. It isn't necessary to have meat or fish every day – you can have cheese instead, for instance – but you do need protein for energy. Fibre in the diet is also important as is iron – especially as we get older. They can be supplied by fresh spinach, liver, eggs, lean meat, currants, raisins and wholemeal bread, for example. If you are a vegetarian then dairy products should form a good part of your diet. And if you are a vegan then fruit, vegetables and pulses are important. Many times headaches and tiredness can be helped by a good meal. Healthy eating is important to our emotional and psychological well-being, too, as the young woman who came to see me found out.

Have a good cookery-book on hand. Years ago I was given a complete Mrs Beeton and I have found it invaluable. Not only does it give good and easy recipes but also helpful household hints. Sainsbury's do a range of cook-books that are inexpensive and helpful, too. These are only two of the many good cookery-books on the market today.

If you are feeling a bit down and are contemplating an evening alone, why not plan to buy your favourite food (providing it doesn't break the budget). Cook it with the trimmings, set your table or tray tastefully, lighting a candle or arranging some flowers, and enjoy it. You're worth it!

Some people hate eating alone. Understandably those who've been married often find eating alone harder to bear than those of us who haven't. If you are one for whom eating alone is a painful experience, try reading. I have dined with many famous people this way! Or plan your meal to coincide with some TV programme you want to watch, or radio programme you particularly want to hear. These can all help alleviate the feeling of being alone.

EATING WITH FRIENDS

Be willing to share your meal – however simple – with another. Singles often complain that they are seldom – if ever – invited out. If this is the case I think we must ask ourselves, 'When did I last invite someone out? What am I doing by way of entertaining others and how much is my home open?' It is so easy to get caught up in self-pity and feel that nobody wants you or likes you because you haven't been invited out for a long time. But if we habitually feel like this we shall not be helping ourselves and we'll probably put people off having us because of not being very good company!

Friendship is a mutual thing and should never be taken for granted. Just before I went to the United States for the first time, to spend a year in training at the headquarters of the Navigators, I remember praying that the Lord would help me to establish a good rapport with the people I should meet. I knew I should not take this for granted, even though I was going to be with other Christians, and very dedicated ones at that.

People sometimes say, 'You must come over and see us.'

Then we may wait a long time for a more definite invitation which may never come at all. We feel let down. Does it ever occur to us that the person who made that statement in all good faith is a busy person, too, and perhaps they are waiting for that 'perfect' time that never comes? Why not phone them one day and say, 'You very kindly said I could come over one day and see you. I should really love to, so may I take you up on your invitation? When would be a convenient time?' I have both done that and had it done to me, when it was I who had given the initial invitation to someone. I really appreciated that person phoning to take me up on my offer because it made me realise that the person wanted to come and see me. Also it stopped me in my business and made me nail down a definite time instead of vaguely thinking, 'I must ask so-and-so soon', and never doing it. We have all been guilty of this at some time or another so let's help each other and not moan about it.

SHARING PRACTICAL PROBLEMS

During a discussion period at a widow's conference which I was leading, one widow told how an elder from her church had come round not long after the death of her husband and had offered to cut the hedge in her front garden. As she gratefully accepted his offer he then went on to say that from then on her hedge would be his responsibility. Not many of the other widows, sadly, could share a similar experience. But it did create a lively discussion about help needed, whether or not people should ask, how we can be observant to others' needs and many similar subjects. In every church today there are many single parents and widowed people and often we realise that their needs are not being met. How many single parents long for someone to take the children for a few hours so that they can get away for a needed break. A young widow in Belfast told how her son had said one day, 'I wish I had a father,' her reply was, 'You have – he's in heaven.' 'I know,' said the boy, 'but I wish I had someone to take me fishing.' How good it would have been if some man in her church had thought to include her son in any fishing trips with his own.

We also discussed the problem that many had about asking for help. Some will not do this through pride or self-sufficiency, but often they are the very ones who complain that the church does nothing for them! How can people help us when they don't know our needs? And the other side of that coin is that anyone offering to help might be afraid of causing offence through implying that we can't cope. So it can become a stalemate with neither side making a move. That was not the practice of the early Church. Needs were made known and needs were met (Acts 4:34-5).

One area where singles often would like help is in the area of finance. A widow has possibly always depended on her husband and is now having to cope alone; single parents often find themselves in very difficult financial straits and are not aware of the financial help they can receive; and many single people have a hard time living within their budget.

I have a friend who is very gifted in matters financial and as a result she has become the financial and tax adviser to many of her friends, myself included. One piece of advice which came as a great relief to me was that if I had financial difficulties and was getting behind with my payments, I should go and discuss it with the people concerned. This is far better than not paying bills and giving our creditors no explanation. Of course, ideally, we should budget and make sure we are not living beyond our incomes, but to all of us at some time comes the unexpected, and this can 'throw us' and mean that we haven't enough to pay a car-repair bill or even the mortgage that month. Admitting this takes courage, but the outcome can be good as I found when I went to my garage and asked for an extra month for the payment of a rather large repair bill. My request was granted, and my relief was great.

If you are experiencing difficulty with your budget, both setting it and living within it, don't be afraid to ask for help. You don't have to find a financial genius to help you, either. A friend whom you trust and who seems to be managing well would probably be only too happy to help you. And remember, when we *ask* for help we are often giving it too. People respond to being needed and in this climate of giving and receiving help, it may be possible for good conversations to take place – perhaps about the Lord – with Christians or non-Christians.

MAKING THE MOST OF HOLIDAYS

Holidays are often very difficult times for singles as they wonder what to do, where to go and with whom to go. The special times like Christmas, Easter and other holidays can be nightmares if not planned in advance. One friend facing her first Christmas following the death of both her parents, and realising she could finish up being alone at home, booked herself a trip to Switzerland through a Christian travel agent who even recommended a good church for her to attend while there. She came back thrilled, having had a very memorable and enjoyable Christmas. Another year she went to a Christian conference centre house-party which she found equally enjoyable.

Neither of these things may fit your pocket or your preference, but my point is that those times need planning for. We always think of Christmas as being a family time, but you can make your home into a 'family' by inviting other singles who are also alone to join you for Christmas, or Easter, sharing the catering and making it as enjoyable as you can. I enjoy decorating my home for Christmas whether I shall be in it on the day or not. I usually get a small Christmas tree and with various trinkets that I have gathered through the years, I have great enjoyment decorating it and making my flat especially attractive and cosy.

What about summer holidays? Pray and plan well in advance. Maybe there is someone with whom you could enjoy the holiday and it would be a mutual blessing. I remember when in nursing training wondering with whom I could go on holiday as several of my friends were already booked. I phoned a girl I hardly knew (we had been bridesmaids together at a friend's wedding and had only met two or three times) and asked her if she would like to come to Italy with me. I think she was a bit surprised, but was also pleased, and we had a very enjoyable time. I knew enough about her before we went to know we had similar interests.

Some people, though, do enjoy going away on their own like another friend of mine who will happily take herself off to a good hotel with her golf-clubs for a week or two. There is also a growing number of very good Christian hotels or conference centres where a person very quickly feels at home even if he or she goes there alone.

DOING CREATIVE, INTERESTING THINGS

Loneliness is often bound up with boredom and we can replace boredom with varied and interesting activities. What about the art of letter-writing! It was recently stated that the average person in Britain writes forty-two letters a year. No wonder some people feel neglected! Letter-writing can be a great ministry and one on which we can all engage. Even a brief note letting someone know we are thinking of them especially, or enquiring to know how they are, may be all that is required.

Some people like to go to art classes; one girl decided to take a motor-mechanic course so she would know what to do if her car broke down.

Finding a live church and joining in weeknight activities or house-groups as well as attending Sunday worship is important, and looking for a job in the church too. How often we hear of overworked clergy unable to get people to do necessary jobs in the church and yet many single people say they are lonely and feel unneeded! Sometimes, I know, it is true that the church often seems to use couples in positions of responsibility more than single people and this is regrettable, but nevertheless it is also true that single people often hold back from either volunteering or starting something on their own such as a home Bible study. One single friend of mine who had no special training and not a lot of experience in leading Bible studies after hosting a religious radio course during Lent in her home, decided to hold a Bible study every other week. The people who came were different in many ways but she asked them to lead in turn, and the outcome was a very successful group and one which was a blessing to her as well as to all its other members.

DEVELOPING DEEP SAME-SEX FRIENDSHIPS

The second time I went to the States, this time to work with Bible Study Fellowship, I expected to be there for several years, so I prayed that God would give me a special friend, outside of my work, with whom I could relax and be myself, someone with whom I could do things and go places. I was also looking for someone with whom I could have real spiritual fellowship. As friendship is a mutual thing I wanted to be able to contribute to her life as much as she would contribute to mine. I prayed for a year and then the Lord provided such a friend. We had great times together as we both had similar interests and we came to understand and accept each other, learning from each other, and being open and honest with each other. We laughed a great deal together and above all shared a rich fellowship in prayer.

But this did not mean we lived in each other's pockets, partly because we lived a 45-minute drive away from each other and we both worked. We had a mutual agreement, too, that good friendships are held in an open hand and are not exclusive; we enjoyed each other's company when together and also enjoyed doing many things on our own or with others. That friendship has lasted and has been mutually enriching.

Ask the Lord for a good friend of the same sex, interests, and above all love for the Lord with whom you can feel totally accepted and understood and with whom you can grow in your knowledge and love of the greatest Friend of all.

RELATING WELL TO THE OPPOSITE SEX

Having talked about the importance of having one really good friend of the same sex, let us move on to think about our relationships with the opposite sex. Christians can be very awkward about this, and the numbers of get-togethers among Christians that I have been to where the men were on one side of the room and the women on the other are too numerous to mention. Happily, it does seem that this kind of thing happens less frequently nowadays.

Many singles are afraid to go out with a member of the opposite sex for various reasons. Some are afraid that the other person might become too serious and then get hurt. Or they are afraid of what other people will say or think when they walk into church, or are seen out with someone of the opposite sex. Many a lovely friendship has been stifled for such reasons or because of thoughtless remarks or questions. 'Is this serious?' we may ask a friend when they go out for the first time with someone. This tactless question may put paid to any future dates. We can't only blame our married friends for these thoughtless remarks because we singles do it to each other, too. I have often felt sorry for people in the limelight whose pictures appear in the papers with a friend above a caption such as: 'Is this the one?' Publicising a private question might mean that the answer turns out to be negative when it might have been positive. So let us watch our own responses and remarks.

A good healthy appreciation and understanding of the opposite sex should not be shunned by singles through fear; nor should they be held back by old-fashioned taboos. Developing healthy friendships with the opposite sex in the teen and college years is to be encouraged. Much can be learned from each other and mutual support and affirmation given and received, and this could prove an important part of the preparation for future lasting relationships. Setting standards of behaviour and sticking to them is very important both as a Christian witness and in order to start marriage in the way that God intended.

As we get older it is sometimes harder – though not impossible – to have platonic friendships. But you will only enjoy such friendships if you avoid the temptation of thinking of everyone you go out with as a potential marriage partner. A man or woman who is obviously looking for a marriage partner can spoil what could have been a very happy friendship as well as frightening people off.

It is true that there are more Christian women than there are men and this has always posed a problem. Whereas one knows and has social contact with non-Christians of the opposite sex, for the Christian man or woman looking for a deeper, though platonic, friendship this should be sought for with a fellow-Christian. Then if things do develop there will not be the danger of being 'unequally yoked' or of having to get out of a situation which should never have arisen.

There are many unhappy marriages where a Christian has knowingly married a non-Christian, sometimes erroneously thinking that, when married, his or her partner will become a Christian. It very seldom works this way – perhaps when we disobey God, we can't expect Him to bless. I should add, however, that when a person recognises and repents of this, God will bless. But any Christian man or woman at present

contemplating marriage to a non-Christian should realise
that this is contrary to God's revealed will. Where two non-
Christians marry and later one becomes a Christian – that is
quite a different matter. It isn't easy then, either, but at least
there wasn't disobedience to God's will.

A lively Christian church with plenty of other single people
would be an obvious place to make Christian friends. Other
places might be Christian conference centres or organisations
like the Navigators and Campus Crusade. Look for a friend
who above all shares your same love for the Lord Jesus Christ
and desires to put Him first.

COPING WITH SEXUAL DESIRES

We have just talked about having friends of the opposite sex.
This will immediately raise the question for some, 'But how
can I cope with the longings and desires for sex that
sometimes seem to overwhelm me?' As we mentioned earlier,
sex was created and given by God and is not something to be
feared or looked upon as anything less than good and
wholesome. God gave it, however, to be used within the
confines of marriage. To have sexual desires is perfectly
normal and being attracted by a beautiful girl or a handsome
man is no more unnatural or wrong than being overcome by
the beauty of a sunset or some lovely music. It is what we do
with these thoughts and feelings that is important. Jesus said
that if a man looked at a woman lustfully he had already
committed adultery with her in his heart (Matt. 5:28).
Sexuality has a great deal to do with our minds and thoughts.
Certainly physiological and hormonal changes in our bodies,
such as those women experience at certain times of the
month, affect us, too. But probably the most important thing
is what we feed our minds on. I remember hearing a sad story
of a clergyman who had to leave his church because of sexual
misconduct. After he had left, pornographic pictures were

found in his desk drawer. This is what he had been feeding his mind with for years – it is small wonder that his actions followed suit.

Earlier on in this chapter I spoke about the importance of feeding our minds with Scripture. I cannot emphasise this too much in this context. When sexual desires sweep over you, remember that they have originated in your mind, so substituting them in the mind with something else is important. And what better than a verse of Scripture, or better yet, a passage of Scripture that has meant a great deal to you. We are often encouraged when tempted to quote the verse, 1 Corinthians 10:13. It is such a long verse that by the time you get to the end the temptation is likely to have gone – you may even have forgotten what it was! But the action of Scripture on the mind not only moves out that which should go but in its place gives healing and positive enrichment. So negatively it casts out wrong and positively it replaces it with good.

Then it is good not to be inactive at such times. Get up and do something; exercise, clean the house or phone someone; do something that will engage your mind and body.

For single Christians relinquishment is the crucial word in relation to sexual relationships and childbearing outside marriage. The worldling will go off and satisfy his desires by hook or by crook; but what good has that done the world or the individual? For the Christian this is not an option. What is open for the Christian is the far greater and more rewarding experience of knowing that if the Lord does not have someone for you now or even in the future He is able to satisfy your desires and make up to you far more than anything you feel you may have lost.

A.W. Tozer in his classic, *The Pursuit of God*, says: '... that God is so vastly wonderful, so utterly and completely delightful that He can, without anything other than Himself, meet and overflow the deepest demands of our total nature, mysterious and deep as that nature is'.

We are not here to please ourselves, we are here on earth to glorify God and to enjoy Him for ever. He has given ample provision for the accomplishment of this if we will only accept it.

DEVELOPING A RICH INNER LIFE

Fundamental to everything that I have said in the last two chapters is the development of a rich, inner life. It is from this that an attractive personality grows; it is this which makes it possible for stumbling-blocks to be turned into stepping-stones.

How much time do you spend on the development of a rich, inner life? Why not, for a week, note what proportion of your time is spent on activities and what proportion on prayer, meditation and reflection? Perhaps your findings will shock you.

Much of what we see and read and hear of as we rush busily about will tend to fill our minds with whatever *isn't* noble, right, pure, lovely, admirable, excellent, praiseworthy (Philippians 4:8). So we need to take time to fill our minds with the opposite things. Do we?

Above all, we need to develop a deep, honest relationship with the Lord, and this will certainly involve much time spent in reading and meditating on the Bible. I should like to emphasise also something which isn't always emphasised enough: the importance of *memorising* Scripture.

Memorising Scripture, so that it can be recalled and applied at the right time, is, I would say, vital in the whole process of inner healing which involves all the layers of our personalities. It isn't only our thoughts that give us problems; what comes from our subconscious into our conscious minds often causes us much pain, too.

These thoughts can come unbidden and overwhelm us. Thoughts of being rejected, unloved, worthless and many other such negatives, need to be replaced by thoughts that repudiate these from the standpoint of truth, and what better place to turn to than Scripture. If it is to change our life the Bible must not only be memorised but also meditated on and obeyed. Memorisation is a most effective way of accomplishing true meditation and subsequent obedience. The thoughts from the Scriptures, well digested, penetrate the subconscious mind and eventually change our thought patterns. 'For as he thinketh in his heart, so is he' (Prov. 23:7AV).

If you want to have the mind of Christ and so become more like Him you need to think His thoughts, and the Scriptures will enable you to do that. A young student, who later was greatly used of God, was told by a lecturer that if she wanted a mind like Shakespeare she needed to read and study Shakespeare. If, on the other hand, she wanted a trashy mind, then she would need to fill it with cheap novels and horror stories. The principle is: 'Rubbish in, rubbish out'. This particular student decided to acquire a mind like the Apostle Paul and spent years studying, memorising and meditating on the Pauline Epistles, as well as all other parts of Scripture. A small wonder that a fruitful and much-used life ensued! Just taking one verse a day from something you have read in your quiet time can be a good way of beginning. Write it down and then commit it to memory and meditate on it during the day as you travel to work, do the household chores, wait for a bus or train. You will be amazed at the amount of time you do have to think, pray or meditate at these moments, yet how often we say we have no time.

In the next chapter we shall consider how we can overcome some of the very natural yet nevertheless devastating fears and worries we can experience – particularly if we have no one with whom to share them.

5

SHADOWS ON THE STAIRCASE
(Dealing with worry and fear)

Shirley went into hospital to have her breast removed – a very traumatic operation for a woman, quite apart from the fear and anxiety of knowing that her body has been invaded by cancer. When it was over and she was quietly recovering from the anaesthetic, a patient in the opposite bed, who was being visited by her husband, said to him about Shirley, 'I've been watching that woman come round from her anaesthetic and I've never seen anyone so peaceful. She's got something and I want to know what it is.' Her wish was granted later – when Shirley explained that what she had was a personal knowledge of Jesus Christ and a deep assurance of His control over the events of her life, and it was this that produced in her a deep sense of peace. As a result Shirley had the joy of leading her fellow-patient to the Lord.

This story is, perhaps, even more striking these days when stress seems so universal. We see worried people hurrying past us in the street, or sitting opposite us in the bus or Underground every day. Books are written on coping with stress, meditation, positive thinking and other allied subjects. But the sort of peace that Shirley had, and which I believe we can all have, is not the product of self-help techniques, however good.

WORRY

Worry is something we all do to a greater or lesser degree. How irritated we feel when someone tritely says to us in the middle of some personal crisis, 'Don't worry. I'm sure it will all work out in the end.' It's so easy for them to say it since they are not involved and the crisis does not affect them. Yet worry and anxiety can be at the root of many physical ailments such as – to mention but a few – ulcers, high blood pressure, insomnia and weight loss or gain.

The worries that single people experience may be different from those of married people; if we are inclined to envy our married friends, we should remind ourselves that we might feel very differently if we were in their shoes carrying their burdens and anxieties.

What is worry?

How do we define worry? One definition could be: Bearing responsibilities that are not ours or about which we can do nothing. That definition could suggest that much of our worrying has to do with the future, and how many of us can control that?

Worry about tomorrow

Jesus said, 'Therefore do not worry about tomorrow, for tomorrow will worry about itself. Each day has enough trouble of its own' (Matt. 6:34). Here again the suggestion is that we tend, mistakenly, to spend time living in the future instead of the present. Not that planning and saving for the future, and using our commonsense are wrong. When in the preceding verses Jesus tells us not to worry about clothes, or food and drink – the necessities of life – He is not saying that we should not dress nicely or buy and cook good food. No, He is saying that we should not have an inordinate concern over these things. In verse 32 He says, 'For the pagans run after all these things...' Acquiring these necessities was a very important part of their lives and a matter of status. This is what Jesus is speaking against. Interestingly, the Greek word for worry in the New Testament has the sense of dividing, parting, ripping or tearing apart. Isn't that an element in intense worry? We feel torn apart. A day in which we feel torn apart can be much more exhausting than a day filled with physical labour; and that gripping fear in the pit of the stomach can also ruin appetite, and, in the end, produce an ulcer which eats away at the lining of the stomach.

Much of our worrying centres on the thought of, 'What will happen if ... ?' Very often the 'if' never happens. Or we think: 'Supposing I get sick, lose my job, can't pay my mortgage ...?' The 'supposes' – which can cause us sleepless nights – may never materialise. Jesus asks the question, 'Who of you by worrying can add a single hour to his life?' (Matt. 6:27). Not only can we not add an hour, but a life of worry can do much to shorten the hours or length of our lives.

Worry is partly linked with temperament and it is true that some temperaments are more of the worrying kind than others. Sanguine and Phlegmatic people (see Chapter Two) would be less likely to worry than those with choleric or melancholic temperaments. But a person who is temperamentally prone to anxiety, doesn't have to resign himself (or herself) to being a chronic worrier for ever. As a Christian it is possible for such a person to overcome this tendency.

Worry can lead to self-pity. It can also lead to inactivity or laziness. Jesus told a parable about an unfaithful steward in Matthew 25 who hid his master's talent because he feared him. He knew him to be a hard man, worried about what to do with the money and ended up doing nothing. The master's response is interesting. 'You wicked, lazy servant!' (v.26). We can be so overcome with anxiety at times that it seems to paralyse us so that we do nothing – nothing, that is, except think about tomorrow's problems!

Worry about yesterday

Another cause of an anxious and troubled spirit can be worrying over yesterday. We think, 'If only I hadn't said this, or done that,' or, 'If only I had applied for that job, or taken that course that would have given better qualifications; written that letter, or phoned my friend at that particular time . . .' But those things are all 'water under the bridge'. No amount of longing can bring them back. No amount of regretting will change the situation. If we dwell on the past we can miss out on the present. Consumed with worry as we look back, we may not notice present good or present opportunities.

Worry and goals

Often our anxieties centre around the pursuing of goals that we don't seem to be able to reach or which others seem to block. We may need to stop and evaluate what these goals are and see whether they are the right goals for us. For example, if my goal for this book is that so many thousands will read it, and this doesn't happen, I shall feel frustrated and have a great sense of failure. If, on the other hand, my goal is that God will be glorified by the book and that there will be blessing and help for those who read it, then even if only one person were to tell me that he or she had been helped, my goal – a much worthier one – would have been reached. We can spend so much time striving and worrying about the wrong sort of goals – those which are beyond us or are not the best for us.

ANTIDOTES TO WORRY

So what can we do about our worrying? How can we deal with our anxiety? I have found the following antidotes to be effective.

Trust in God's power

First of all, in combating worry, we need to remind ourselves, as we already thought about in Chapter One, that God is in control. He is in charge of both our life in the present and in the future. Tomorrow belongs to God, so when we worry about the future we are stealing something that belongs to Him.

Corrie ten Boom tells how her father helped her to gain peace in facing the terrible ordeal of going into a concentration camp. She wondered if she would be able to endure, and many frightening thoughts must surely have filled her mind. Tenderly, her father asked her to recall the times in her childhood when she went off on her own to visit her grandmother and he would accompany her to the station. Then he asked, 'Corrie, when would I give you the ticket?' She replied, 'When I had boarded the train.' Her father then pointed out that God gives us His strength when we need it, not before, so there is little point in worrying beforehand about how we shall cope with a situation.

We need to remind ourselves that God is indeed 'the Blessed controller of all things' (1 Tim. 6:15 Phillips). If we have committed our lives to Him and our chief desire is to do His will, then we can confidently expect the Lord to work things out for us even at times when the situation looks confusing and is frustrating. How often have we found that something we hoped would happen didn't – much to our annoyance, perhaps – and then later realised that God had worked everything (including the disappointment) together for good?

When I first joined the staff of the Navigators in Britain I hoped and prayed earnestly that I would be sent to their headquarters, Glen Eyrie, in Colorado Springs. This would not only have fulfilled a lifelong ambition, namely to go to the States, but also I felt that to begin my training at the very centre of an organisation and to see its inner workings would be extremely helpful. But that was not the way the organisation worked. And so for five years I worked in England while continuing to make my request! When eventually I did go to Glen Eyrie, I knew God's timing had been right.

Rejoice in God's goodness

Praise and thanksgiving are probably the most effective ways of reducing worry and stress. I am sure that you have found, as I have, that if faced with a difficult job or trying situation, I start to complain about it, it becomes ten times worse and my performance becomes correspondingly less effective. If, on the other hand, I praise God even for the difficult situation because of all that I can learn through it, and so face it in a more relaxed way, this makes all the difference in the world. It is not that the situation changes, but my attitude changes and so I am able to cope with the problem.

Paul, writing from prison to the Philippians, said, 'Do not be anxious about anything, but in everything, by prayer and petition, with thanksgiving, present your requests to God. And the peace of God, which transcends all understanding, will guard your hearts and your minds in Christ Jesus' (Phil. 4:6-7). Paul was not only imprisoned but also uncertain about how much longer he had to live. What anxious care he could have had – for himself, the churches, friends, loved ones! Many pressures could have crowded in on him but they didn't. Instead he experienced peace which passed all understanding. The world cannot understand when we have peace in the middle of a crisis, so no wonder we – like Shirley – get asked the question, 'What is your secret?'

Develop a spirit of thankfulness

In order to develop a spirit of thankfulness, we may well need to reprogramme our thoughts and have to admit that we are worriers. Then we need to recognise God's sovereignty in our lives and affairs, and thank Him for it. And if we go on saying 'Thank you' to God, we shall be helping ourselves to develop a spirit of thankfulness. What if we don't feel thankful? Isn't it hypocritical to obey a command of God's when your feelings don't match what you're doing? I believe we should obey with our will and having done that often our feelings will follow. In God's word we read, 'give thanks in all circumstances, for this is God's will for you in Christ Jesus' (1 Thess. 5:18) – a command not often obeyed, I think. The verse doesn't say *'for* all circumstances', but *'in* all circumstances'. So I won't say 'Lord, thank you that I've broken my leg,' but 'I thank you, Lord, that even in this situation which You have allowed, You will be with me to help me and to bring glory to Your name'. Being thankful helps us to relax in the situation and this is conducive to healing, both physical and emotional, and enables the power of God to flow through us in blessing. We shall consider more about quietness and relaxation in another chapter, but it is very important in our overcoming anxiety.

Share the problem with God

Don't be afraid to be completely honest with the Lord. David was, as we see from so many of the Psalms. I suspect that one of the reasons for which the Psalms are so popular, is that they cover the whole gamut of emotions from the highest praise and thanksgiving to the deepest depression.

Compare Psalm 103 with Psalm 22 for example. God knows exactly what we are thinking before we tell Him. You might ask 'Why tell Him how I feel if He already knows that?' The answer – or part of it, anyway – is that it does me good to do this. Bottling things up inside us can be like sitting on a bomb which one day explodes. So our unexpressed feelings or thoughts may explode into ulcers, high blood pressure, heart attacks or strokes: as we said earlier, it is the unacknowledged emotions that cause the problems. And who better to express our feelings and emotions to than God? Verbalise your feelings to Him, and don't be afraid. You can't shock Him.

Being in Christian work is not a bed of roses, and on one occasion I worked with a colleague who had a very difficult temperament and a dominating personality. At that stage of my life, in my early thirties, I found it hard to stand up to a strong personality and hold on to my convictions. This particular person enjoyed arguments and making others think and evaluate motives. The latter is no bad thing, but unfortunately the approach was very dogmatic and somewhat belligerent. After many months of enduring this – not very well, I'm afraid – I found myself getting nowhere in praying for this person and in my attitude and relationship with her. Matters became worse and worse. Then one day I decided I had better be honest with God! Instead of saying my usual little prayer, first telling the Lord that I did love her but . . . I decided to come right out with it and say what was really in my heart! 'Lord, I hate her. I'm sorry but that is the fact.' I had hardly finished saying just that when I felt an enormous sense of relief, almost as though the Lord was saying to me, 'At last you have been honest and admitted what I have known all along. Now I can help you.' And He did. The situation didn't change and things continued to be difficult, but I now felt free to learn from the experience instead of being intimidated by it. Years later when I met this person again, we were able to meet on a healed and restored footing.

Sometimes it's helpful to write down what we are feeling. This can help us to discover what is causing the worry, takes away that nebulous feeling of unease and brings the problem into clear focus. Then we should take the matter specifically to the Lord – spreading out before Him the paper on which we have written our problems and presenting it to Him, much as Hezekiah did with his disturbing letter (Isa. 37:14). As we pray it through (which isn't the same as worrying it through), but praying perhaps out loud, we can ask Him what He would have us do.

Very often I have found at such times that the first thing that happens, before the Lord ever shows me what He wants me to do, is that a deep peace comes into my heart. I cannot emphasise strongly enough how important this peace is. I would even suggest that we should not get up from our knees until that peace has been gained, because that is the climate in which we can hear what God is saying to us. We wouldn't be able to hear Him while the clamour of our anxiety is noisily taking control. We need to have a quiet mind and heart and God can give those to us if we would but give Him the problem and by an act of the will hand it – however big or frightening – over to Him. When we are quiet and at peace, the Lord can show us how to act and what to say.

Having discovered that, we need to obey. The next step might be to write down when, where and how you will begin, and then be sure you keep to it. By doing that you break out of the gripping vice of inertia that worry produces and which in itself adds to the anxiety, as the very act of commencing on a course of action in itself does something to lessen the grip of anxiety.

Committing to memory such verses as Philippians 4:6,7; Isaiah 26:3, 32:17,18, 33:5,6; John 15:11, 16:33 helps not only to focus the mind on peace but on the source of peace.

As well as sharing our worries with God, we can share them with our friends. We must be careful, however, to choose the right friends for this purpose. Some people, by what they say, make us feel rather more than less worried by the time we have finished talking to them! This is often experienced by patients in a hospital ward talking with their fellow-sufferers. Some people love to recount all the gory details and any complications that might follow or that they or their friends might have experienced.

FEAR

Following on from worry comes the even more chilling emotion of fear. There are many types of fear: fear of people's opinion, something which affects us all to a greater or lesser degree, fear of illness, death, the unknown, failure, loneliness, accident, violence (a growing fear today). And then there are irrational fears – feelings of dread and panic which have no basis in reality.

Not all fear is bad, of course. Some is the God-given fear that is part of our self-preservation drive. It is sensible of me to fear that if I rush blindly out into the road I will get knocked down and run over. Then there is the reverential 'fear' we are to have of God and of displeasing Him and doing wrong. These are all perfectly natural and healthy fears.

It is significant that one of the most frequently repeated commands in the Bible is the command to 'fear not'. It has been said that there are 366 such commands in the Bible, one for every day of the year plus leap year. Why is this commandment repeated so often? Could it be because fear can be not only a crippling paralysing emotion, but also a dangerous one in that it can cause us to act and speak in ways that can cause great harm. Surely all of us at some time in our lives have lied through fear, or only told half the truth. We have failed to do something we know we should have done through fear, perhaps because of what others might think of us. Peter denied his Lord, and the other disciples who had also been His constant companions for three years fled at the moment of crisis through fear.

Fear of other people's opinions

Perhaps one of the chief causes of fear in our daily lives is the fear of what people will say to us or about us. 'Will I be accepted?' 'Will friends criticise me for this or that?' 'What will people say if I buy that rather expensive-looking car?'

In Proverbs 29:25 we are told, 'Fear of man will prove to be a snare, but whoever trusts in the Lord is kept safe.' Through Isaiah, the Lord reminds us that He comforts us, gently chiding us for our fear which has made us forget that the Almighty Creator God has all things, even the 'wrath of the oppressor', under His control (Isa. 51:12,13).

Fear of violence

Many people living alone today, fear violence. If this fear prompts them to get good locks on their doors and windows and make sure they lock up carefully at night then that is good – they are being good stewards of their lives and property. But what then? Then they need to cast themselves upon the Lord and count on His presence and care continually.

I remember some years ago travelling in a non-corridor train and finding myself seated opposite a rather sinister-looking man who fixed his eyes menacingly on me. There was no one else in the compartment and no way, in between stations, of escaping from it and I had visions of finishing up as another murder or rape statistic! I tried looking away out of the window, but I was conscious of his continued gaze and I felt very scared, especially as it was getting dark. So I prayed like this: 'Lord Jesus, please stand between me and this man and protect me.' It was quite miraculous to me that in a matter of seconds after that prayer the man for the first time averted his gaze and looked out of the window. At the next station, he got out of the train. I felt very protected and very conscious of the Lord's presence.

Since then I have several times prayed that the Lord would be a protection between me and someone or something. While I was living in California, for example, my next-door neighbour was mugged and had her handbag snatched as she walked up the steps to her apartment one evening. It shook all of us who were living near by and I was especially concerned because I knew that a few nights later I would be coming home alone at around midnight. On that night I drove down our deserted street praying, and was thinking about what lay in store for me – a lonely walk up two flights of stairs before reaching my apartment. Just as I was about to drive into the carport, I was surprised to see, in the middle of the road a large Alsatian dog. He was simply standing there. I had never seen him before and had no idea where he could have come from. I turned my car in, got out and locked up and there he was standing right by my car. I went to stroke him and he backed away. As I started up my stairs he followed me and came right with me to the front door of my apartment. When I got there, I turned to him and said, 'It's all right now, you can go home.' With that, he turned tail and ran off. I never saw that dog again. You may draw your own conclusions. As far as I was concerned, God answered my prayer for protection!

But it would be wrong to suggest that Christians are immune from being attacked or murdered. I have written earlier in this book about two Christian women who were raped and there are other similar stories. Does God, at times, withdraw His protecting hand from us as he appeared to do with Job? I believe the devil delights to put such fears into our minds, causing us to doubt God's goodness or power. No wonder Paul writing to Timothy said, 'For God hath not given us the spirit of fear; but of power, and of love, and of a sound mind' (2 Tim. 1:7AV). Those sorts of fears are not from God but from Satan and we need to withstand him and the fear as we would any sin.

Fear of failure

What about fear of failure? This is probably tied up with fear of what people will say. But as well as this there is the fear that we shall be unsuccessful.

We need to realise that everyone fails some of the time and

that failure can bring positive good. What big-headed people many of us would be if we lived our lives in continual success! Some of the greatest qualities of character are acquired, and some of life's deepest and most important lessons are learned, as a result of failure. 'But,' you may say, 'failure isn't a once in a while thing, with me; it seems to be continual!' Is it really? Or have you slipped into a failure mentality? Are you really thinking clearly? Have you made a generality out of a few failures? It might be worth while to think back over your life. Aren't there times when you felt a failure but needn't have – because things worked out for the best in the end? I know this happens to me at times. I chide myself mercilessly for not making a phone call or doing something else – only to find out later that it was just as well that I hadn't made that call or done that thing. At other times, of course, I chide myself for my failure and I'm quite right to do so. Yet facing up to the fact of failure can be the beginning of learning from it.

OVERCOMING FEAR

In Romans 8 Paul also reminds us that nothing will ever be able to separate us from God's love so perfectly demonstrated in Christ's death. Even when bad things do happen to us, we are not to conclude that God does not love us or that he has deserted us (v.35 Living Bible). Evil may come to us living as we do in an evil world, but even when it does we can be 'more than conquerors through him who loved us' (Rom. 8:37) by experiencing God's peace and grace in new, unimagined ways.

At a practical level, there may be things we can do to dispel or lessen our fears. As with anxiety, it is sometimes helpful to write down our fears so that we can see if there is any specific action we can take. Some people spend a long time being afraid that they have cancer, or some other disease, when a visit to the doctor would either dispel the fear (which often happens) or confirm it (in which case the sooner this happens, the greater the likelihood of a good outcome through appropriate treatment). We can save ourselves weeks or months of agonising fear and this may have a bearing on our recovery.

If you live alone it's obviously sensible to have locks on doors and windows, and to lock up early. It is also sensible to get to bed reasonably early because sitting up late and especially, perish the thought, watching late-night horror movies can produce or exacerbate fear and anxiety. It's late at night, when everyone else is likely to be in bed, that one is usually more conscious of 'the things that go bump in the night!' So trying to go to bed and get to sleep reasonably early is sound advice.

Praying through some of the Psalms like 27, 34, 91, 121, 127, either alone of with a friend can be of the greatest help in removing fear and creating peace. I and many others have experienced this.

Making the most of all God's gifts

So far I have suggested some ways in which we can combat or overcome fear and worry through our relationship with the Lord. But as well as (though certainly not instead of) drawing on spiritual resources, we can make use of the skill and knowledge which God gives to people to help prevent or cure some of the symptoms of fear and worry. As well as fitting in with all that has been learned about healthy living (which is simply part of accepting and co-operating with the way God made us and the world), we can benefit (if appropriate) from therapy, medication, counselling, relaxation, Biblical meditation and so on. These things can be valuable aids in helping us to put worry and fear back where they belong: as servants, not masters. They are useful if they alert us to real dangers or make us take sensible precautions or make sensible plans, but if they serve no useful purpose and are nameless and groundless, or if they rob us of our ability to enjoy life and function properly, then God wants us, I believe, to find in Him and what He provides the resources for growing into clear-sighted confident living.

SUMMARY

Jesus gave us a great mandate for dealing with fear and worry when He said, 'Come to me, all you who are weary and burdened, and I will give you rest. Take my yoke upon you and learn from me, for I am gentle and humble in heart, and you will find rest for your souls. For my yoke is easy and my burden is light' (Matt. 11:28-30).

Much of our worry and fear comes from striving after 'things', the desire to win approval of others, fear of what might happen if ... which stems from a lack of real trust and abandonment to God. Jesus here is telling us to cast ourselves upon Him, and the very key here seems to be the phrase 'for I am gentle and humble in heart'. Jesus seemed to have no fear concerning what people thought or said of Him, or whether God really loved Him or would let Him down in the end. Because of His total abandonment to His Father's will He knew more than anyone else has ever done that total peace and serenity which come from total trust. Is that beyond us? I don't think so because Jesus tells us to learn of Him, and in so doing we shall find rest for our souls. He also tells us to take His yoke upon us, to be willing to be joined together with Him, as in the Old Testament picture of two oxen being yoked together for ploughing. The yoke was made to be a perfect fit so that there was no chafing or rubbing and Jesus goes on to say that His yoke is easy, and His burden that He puts on us is light. What peace to know that the events of our lives are ordered by Him, our loving Lord, that He is our protector and Saviour, and nothing takes Him by surprise. And as we walk with Him, in step with Him, we shall find the striving and vying with others will drop from us. What a rest that brings!

In the next chapter we shall look more closely at our relationship with the Lord, which is the very centre and key to all that we have said thus far about our lives as singles.

6

THERE'S ALWAYS SOMEONE TO TURN TO
(The source and secret of the fulfilled single life)

The church was packed on that evening as I rather reluctantly walked in and took a seat towards the back. I was at a crisis in my Christian life. I had been a Christian for about two years, but had not progressed very much. I had done little or no study of the Bible, and my times of prayer and quiet were few and far between. Also I had been getting more and more involved with worldly ways and people. I had had a non-Christian boyfriend with whom I had become quite serious. This relationship had now ended and I knew that that was right, but I still had the sense of having lost my first love for the Lord; and at the same time there was a conflict going on inside me: I wanted to follow the Lord and yet baulked at the discipline and the commitment.

The talk that evening seemed totally directed at me. I felt that God had brought me to this place against my will, but very much in His purpose. I don't remember much about the meeting, or even the speaker's name, but I do remember that his message was based on the verse, 'For to me, to live is Christ' (Phil. 1:21). I was challenged and convicted.

When the meeting ended, I wanted to slip away without speaking to anyone. So I got up and began to leave. The preacher was already at the door greeting people. I had no intention of speaking to him. I was rather shy at that stage of my life; besides, what would I say? As I moved out through the door, I noticed he was busy talking to someone, so felt that I was quite safe. Suddenly I was shattered and rooted to the spot, as he excused himself to the person to whom he had been speaking and put his hand out to me. As I took it he said, 'For to me, to live is . . .' and waited. I knew the answer, but I struggled. Could I really say it and mean it – because I knew I shouldn't say it unless I meant it. The battle raged. But I knew deep down what I wanted to say. I finished the sentence as I shook his hand: 'Christ,' I said. He smiled and said, 'God bless you,' and I stepped out into the still night air.

As I walked home I knew I had made the most strategic decision of my life since my conversion. Christ was to be *Lord* of my life, not just my Saviour. I remember thinking as I walked home, 'I want to go all the way with Jesus and never turn back.' That has been my desire ever since and the verse in Philippians that has meant so much to me since then, as well as the one mentioned, expresses how I feel: 'I want to know Christ and the power of his resurrection and the fellowship of sharing in his sufferings, becoming like him in his death' (Phil. 3:10).

We come now to the very centre and key to the whole question of living a fulfilled single life: our relationship with the Lord.

As we mentioned in Chapter Two, we have been made physical, mental (emotional) and spiritual beings. If we only operate on the physical and mental planes we are not fully functioning. We are really only half alive. There is a drive in human beings to find identity, peace and deep inner fulfilment. We see many people vainly trying in all kinds of ways to accomplish this goal, which seems to elude them at every turn. So how can they find what they are seeking?

OPENING THE DOOR

A beautiful word-picture gives us the beginning of the

answer. Interestingly it comes in the last book of the Bible, in
the closing act of the greatest drama of all time. There a
picture is given of Christ standing at a door, calling and
knocking for entrance. This picture (Rev. 3:20), although
referring in context to a church which has become lukewarm
in its love and commitment to the Lord and thereby calling
forth a severe rebuke, is nevertheless often used to help
people who are wanting to invite Christ into their heart and
life for the first time. We all need to do this if we are to know
His salvation and come to know Him personally. In inviting
Jesus into our lives, we are acknowledging the fact that we are
sinners and that we accept His death on the cross for our sins.
And when He does enter, He kindles the flame of our spiritual
life – previously we were 'dead in our transgressions and sins'
(Eph. 2:1). Having accepted and received Jesus (about which
I said more in Chapter Two), we need to develop a growing
and fulfilling relationship with Him – which is the subject of
this chapter. This relationship is sometimes spoken of as
'abiding in Christ'.

ABIDING IN CHRIST

What do we mean by abiding in Christ? When Jesus taught
His disciples about this (John 15), He gave a graphic word-
picture of a fruitful vine representing Himself, with the
branches representing believers. Because the branches are
part of the vine and the sap – the very life blood of the vine –
travels up through the main stem and out to the extremities of
each branch, fruit is borne. This is but a natural outcome of
being part of the vine. If a branch were cut off, or if, for some
reason, the sap from the vine was stopped from getting out to
it, no fruit would be borne on that branch.

How does that apply to believers in Christ? When we
receive Christ into our hearts not only does He become part
of us but also we become part of Him. We become a branch of

Him the vine. The sap (the Holy Spirit) flows from the vine into us giving us nourishment, and the ability to be fruitful.

What is this fruit? First, it is the fruit of the Spirit as described in Galatians 5:22-3; these Christ-like qualities will be produced in us little by little. If our lives never show any evidence of such fruit, people could hardly be blamed for questioning whether Christ is really present in our lives or not. 'Thus, by their fruit you will recognise them' (Matt. 7:20) were Jesus' own words. And a Christ-centred life will produce Christ-like qualities.

It will also be effective for God – leading people to Christ or drawing them closer to Him. Some who seldom have the joy of seeing someone respond to the call of Christ then and there and enter the Christian family, are nevertheless faithful in conveying the Gospel and can be valuable links in different chains. Whenever we touch another person's life and help that person to come closer to the Lord, we are being fruitful. Some Christians are particularly gifted in encouraging and building up fellow-believers and there are many who would owe their growth and perhaps leadership in later years, to such persons. What a fruitful ministry that is! Someone once said, 'Your life is your ministry,' meaning that all that we are 'speaks' for the Lord, as well as what we say. Jesus said that even a cup of cold water given to someone in His Name is a ministry that will be blessed.

I was talking along these lines with a friend when I was in the process of writing this chapter. She had been very active in Christian work for many years. At one point in her life, she told me, she had found herself forced to be inactive because of ill-health and was unable to do anything except listen to and encourage her elderly widowed mother. This, she admitted, had been very hard, but she had been able to accept it as her ministry for the time being, just as important then as her previous ministry – that of leading Bible studies and discipling individuals – had been in its time. Prayer is another important and often overlooked ministry. What fruitful lives some elderly or shut-in believers have had over the years as they have prayed for the work of God in different parts of the world!

Christians often shy away from these verses in John 15 thinking that because they are not evangelists regularly leading people to Christ and helping them to commit their lives to Him, they are unfruitful. This is not so. But there are unfruitful Christians. How does this happen?

BLOCKS TO FRUITFULNESS

If a blockage were to occur in a branch, the sap would not be able to flow through and therefore the branch would be unfruitful. Unconfessed sin, deliberate disobedience to the Lord, turning away from Him, perhaps by neglect of prayer and Bible reading – these are the kinds of block which stops us bearing spiritual fruit as we could and should. These things don't cut us out of the vine – they don't nullify our relationship with Jesus which is eternally secure. But they do break temporarily our fellowship with Him, although He continues to abide in us. And when this happens any ministry we are seeking to do becomes mechanical and of the flesh, and no lasting fruit will be produced.

How, in practice and in detail, can we continually abide in Him?

MAKING CHRIST LORD

The starting-point of our real growth in Christ is the surrender of ourselves. If we are really to know God, and His will for our lives, we need to 'offer yourselves as living sacrifices, holy and pleasing to God ...' (Rom. 12:1). Verse 2 goes on to tell us. 'Do not conform any longer to the pattern of this world, but be transformed by the renewing of your mind. Then you will be able to test and approve what God's will is – his good, pleasing and perfect will.'

We surrender ourselves to God by recognising and accepting His sovereignty, accepting our own worth, and acknowledging His goodness to us. We need to give up the right to ourselves – the right to marry, be happy, wealthy and wise. These are not rights in any case; they are gifts from God. We need to realise that, and, hard though it may be, accept it.

WORKING AT INNER QUIETNESS

When I was in nurses' training, I remember our tutor in the course instructing us on the importance of observation for the nurse, saying that we could only be observant if we were quiet inside.

There is a sense in which inner quietness, or peace, is God's gift to those who make Jesus Lord, give up their rights and live to obey and please Him. This is the peace which the world cannot understand or give or take away.

In another sense we need to work at inner quietness. How? By doing all we can to rid our lives and minds of those things not conducive to inner quietness. For example, bitterness, wrath, anger, brawling, slander and malice: these we are to put away from us, Paul tells us (Eph. 4:31). Do we do that? In all honesty, are our church fellowships free of such things?

As well as what is going on in our minds, the actions of our body can be conducive or not to inner peace. If we tend to rush from one thing to the next and crowd as much as we can into our day, we will often find ourselves feeling frantic. Perhaps you are the sort of person who loves to see how much he or she can do before leaving for that appointment and who then arrives late because the last thing undertaken was just one thing too much or took longer than anticipated. I used to be like this and so would feel anxious as I travelled to my appointment at the last moment, and then frustrated and annoyed at being late (if I was); all this quite apart from the annoyance caused to the person I was meeting. So the appointment would not get off to a good start.

I now realise that it is very selfish and seems arrogant to be late and keep someone else waiting because it looks as though we consider our time to be more valuable than the other person's. Have we the right to think like this? Surely someone else's time is as valuable to them as our time is to us; and being on time (or late) expresses courtesy (or discourtesy) to the person or people we are meeting.

Trying to do several jobs at once is probably counter-productive and certainly unhelpful as far as creating the right conditions for inner peace is concerned. Yet it is perfectly possible to do a tremendous amount and still radiate peace. A friend of mine who has a very busy public ministry, speaking at meetings all over the country, in addition to running a home, and being an active member of her church, is nevertheless one of the most peaceful and restful people I know. I love being with her because of this aura of peace. It seems to rub off on to the people she is with. One day I asked her for her secret. I knew that it stemmed mainly from her relationship with the Lord, but there had to be something else because other equally committed Christians whom I knew did not have this peace.

My friend's answer was, 'I don't rush, but give myself plenty of time to do things, or get to places: and I try never to leave things to the last minute!' That taught me a lot.

Noise raises the level of tension in our bodies and blaring radios or television, as well as constantly talking, shouting people can be the culprits here. Sometimes it takes someone else's comment to help us to realise the way we sound. Someone once said to me, after hearing me talk on the phone to a third person, 'If you could lower the pitch and tone of your voice you wouldn't sound so hectic!' Point taken!

If you are a person prone to panic in a crisis, stop and pray, asking God for quietness, before you say or do anything else.

God is far greater than your problems and He never panics. Only when you are at peace can God show you the solution. Sometimes our tension blocks the channel through which He would speak to us.

God often wants to speak to us through the still small voice and we need to be quiet inside to hear that kind of voice. If we feel God is not answering our prayers – prayers for guidance, perhaps – could it be that we are not still or quiet enough for us to hear Him speak to us in our hearts? And perhaps without determination and effort or discipline we never shall be.

MAINTAINING DISCIPLINE

In this permissive age, the word discipline is unpopular. Even among some Christians you can make yourself unpopular by talking about being disciplined in having a quiet time, or in exercising self-denial. The thought of fasting from certain pleasures or from food in order to spend more time in prayer would be considered fanatical by some. I have heard of missionary candidates asking if they could go out into the field to see if they like it before making a definite commitment. Paul's injunction to Timothy to 'Endure hardness like a good soldier of Christ Jesus' (2 Tim. 2:3 AV) is apparently considered to be too frightening and too off-putting for the disciple of the 80s. Much of our evangelism and teaching today avoids this emphasis. Is it any wonder that we are making so little impact on the world and that thousands still are unreached by the Gospel? And is it any wonder, also, that there are many Christians who are unsatisfied with the Christian life because they are living to please themselves and not the Lord?

Discipline must be an important part of our Christian lives if we are to grow. Without discipline we tend to do what we feel like and as a result the essentials of our faith can get .

missed out. For example, how often do you feel like praying, reading, sharing your faith with others? Probably not very often. But prayer and Bible reading should be a daily exercise. They are as vital to the Christian as food is for the body. And witnessing is a command, not an optional extra (Matt. 28:18-20).

The very word *disciple* means *learner*, so we could say that inherent in the word is the idea of disciplined learning. All too often we are undisciplined learners because we are un-disciplined livers! We are quick to express our frustration over unanswered prayer or to complain of our lack of joy in God's word. But what do we *do* about it? Probably the *last* thing we do is to get up half an hour earlier each morning to read the Bible and yet this would make a tremendous difference to our prayer and our joy – among other things. To get up earlier and apply ourselves in this way requires discipline. Are we willing to bear the cost of this?

STUDYING GOD'S WORD

If we are to get beyond merely being acquainted with people we shall need to spend time with them, – in order to discover their interests and how they 'tick'. When we spend a great deal of time with someone, getting to know him really well we often take on some of that person's characteristics. To put it colloquially, something of those whom we admire and like tends to rub off on us. So if we spend much time with the Lord, really making Him our ideal and His word, the Bible, our study, something of Him will rub off on to us. How wonderful!

Through the Scriptures God has communicated His love seen strongly in the Old Testament as well as the New, His justice and holiness and His plan in history. The Bible is rich in poetry and prose, teaching and revelation, but above all it speaks to us of God and by it we grow in our Christian faith (1

Pet. 2:2). Therefore we need to study and meditate on it and make it a part of our lives and beings. I have found it helpful, after reading my Bible passage, to choose a key verse on which to latch my thoughts for the day. If you do this, you will be amazed, as I was, at how much time you can find for meditating on that verse while hoovering, dusting, driving, sitting in a traffic jam, or waiting for an appointment or for a bus or train. Many moments that could otherwise be wasted, can be spent in profitable meditation leading to a deeper knowledge of the Lord.

PLANNING A QUIET TIME

It sounds obvious, but perhaps it needs to be said that if you are going to have a quiet time you need to plan for one! First decide on a time. I would suggest first thing in the morning where this is possible. For parents, especially single parents, this might not be a good time, but for the rest of us, the early-morning hour before the rush of the day sets in, is an ideal time to read and meditate on God's word as well as to pray and commit the day to Him. If we rush pell-mell into the day with no forethought and no preparation – no wonder things get hectic and out of control! I once heard someone say that Christians who do not have a quiet time in the morning are like an orchestra which plays a symphony first and then tunes up afterwards. Amusing but true, perhaps.

The next decision concerns the place. Where will you be able to be quiet and private and reasonably comfortable?

Then comes the strategy – your moment by moment plan. I find it helpful to get out of bed and make a strong cup of tea or coffee. Some people would then wash and dress so as to be thoroughly awake before reading and praying. Whatever you decide concerning these things – do them!

Initially you may want to read a verse of a hymn or psalm or part of a devotional book like *Daily Light* to focus your thoughts on the Lord. Then a brief prayer that you will hear and be guided by Him, before turning to your Bible portion is helpful. Many people find that using daily Bible-reading notes is helpful. Not only do these suggest what to read but they also give a helpful commentary on the reading. Others prefer to choose their own passage and make their own notes. Whichever method you use, stay with it for a time. Avoid the habit of flitting from one portion to another or opening your Bible at random. If you decide, for example, to read St John's Gospel finish it – reading a chapter or half a chapter a day. After that you may want to take an Old Testament book and read that through to the end. Sometimes reading in a translation different from the one you normally use can be stimulating.

How much you read each day will depend on the length of your quiet time, but I would stress that the most important thing is not how much you read but the depth and quality of your reading. It is much better to read five or six verses and have them mean something to you than a whole chapter that you forget almost the moment you finish reading it. Don't be afraid to underline in your Bible or to write neat notes in the margin. This is a way of making the Bible yours and can be of great blessing to you later on when you read what you have written.

It is also helpful to have a small notebook with you as you read and to put into it your key verse for the day – the verse which has really spoken to you and upon which you want to meditate during the day. Memorising such a verse is also an excellent idea.

Then turn to prayer. Begin by praising God for all He is and all He means to you, in other words worship Him. You could use a hymn or psalm to do this. If you live alone you could sing aloud! Do whatever you feel comfortable with, but praise God anyway! Then thank Him for what he has done for you, including some recent blessings, such as the gift of the new day or a good night's sleep (if appropriate). After that commit to God your day and all that you know you will be doing. I like to pray through appointments I may have, or particular work projects I am facing that day, and ask His help. Pray for family members, work colleagues, friends and other people or needs that are in your heart. Not just, 'Lord bless so and so...' Be more specific. If you don't know these people's needs you can always pray through one of the prayers of Paul (e.g. Eph. 3:14-20; Phil. 1:9-11; Col. 1:9-11). There Paul makes specific requests within the general themes of blessing for the believers. As we make similar requests for ourselves and others, we shall, I believe, see them answered. Praying aloud is helpful as it helps to keep our thoughts concentrated, but if you lack the privacy to do this, you can learn to concentrate for silent prayers.

It is important to realise that prayer is not just us talking to God; it is also listening to Him, so we do need to spend some of our prayer time being quiet before Him; 'Be still, and know that I am God' (Ps. 46:10) is a much neglected command and we are the losers if we are disobedient in this respect.

BENEFITING FROM MEDITATION

I have already referred to meditation, but I want to explain what I mean by this word. Meditation involves a verse or passage of Scripture and chewing it over to draw out all the 'meat'. We can begin by asking basic questions such as: What does this mean? What did it mean to the people to whom it was written? What am I going to do about it? Visualising a scene and imagining yourself there can also be a way of meditating. Visualise, for example, the marriage at Cana. Imagine the smell of the food and the chatter of the guests. Watch the host panicking when he realises the wine has run out. Empathise with the feelings of the servants when they are told to fill the pots with water and pour this out as if it were wine. Picture their amazement at discovering that the water

has turned into wine, and their close attention from that
moment to Jesus, who has brought this about. Using our
imagination in this way can bring a story to life and help us to
see it from the inside.

Meditation draws our hearts, our minds and our whole
beings to the Lord in such a way that He can speak and
minister to us. It helps us to develop that inner quietness
which we need – for mental and physical health as well as for
spiritual renewal.

Any single person who wants to live a fulfilled life needs to
learn – in the ways I have suggested and perhaps many others
– to practise the presence of God and to draw on His
resources. There can be no real loneliness when the Lord's
companionship is enjoyed; knowing that we have been made
in the image of God and given a part to play in His plans for
the world bestows meaning and worth on our lives; abiding in
Christ and drawing on the power of His Holy Spirit results in
fruitfulness and increasing Christ-likeness.

Coming to know the Lord in a deeper way means that we
have much to give to a needy world. Jesus said to His
disciples, 'The harvest is plentiful but the workers are few.
Ask the Lord of the harvest, therefore, to send out workers
into his harvest field' (Matt. 9:37-8). One of the advantages of
being single may be that we are, in a special way, free to serve
– something I want to expand in the next chapter.

7

FREE TO SERVE
(Are you available?)

Perhaps one of the greatest advantages of the single life is freedom – freedom to come and go as much as we please without having to consult with husband, wife or children. We are free to travel and live abroad unless there are elderly parents who need our care, although I do not feel that it should be taken for granted that the care of elderly relatives should fall to the lot of the single, and I shall write more about this later.

THE PRICE OF FREEDOM

But freedom does have responsibility. One day I shall have to account for how I used my freedom. Have I been selfishly indulgent, living to please myself, wasting my time? Have I spent my time wallowing in self-pity about my single state or about some problem that I feel is peculiarly and perhaps unfairly mine? In this book I have tried to stress the positive side of singleness and to show that it is possible as a single to live a fulfilled life.

One of the keys to a fulfilled life is a willingness to give ourselves for others. Jesus said, 'For whoever wants to save his life will lose it, but whoever loses his life for me will find it'

(Matt. 16:25). Jesus recognised that there would be sacrifice somewhere. Either we give ourselves to the things of this world and lose the eternal, or we put first the things of God and gain spiritual riches and true fulfilment. We find our real identity and meaning when God has first place in our lives. Our personality can have full expression when we allow Him to direct our lives and purpose. The same applies in marriage – something which often today is overlooked. Perhaps it's the failure to realise that in Christian marriage both individuals need to give themselves to God first and then to each other that has caused so many marriage breakdowns. I think it is good for those of us who are single to remember that we are not the only ones called to make sacrifices!

OUR TRUE IDENTITY

We often hear it said today that people are searching for identity ... who am I and where am I going? What is, or should be, my contribution in the world? If we have the wrong expectations of our own identity or contributions we could end up feeling totally frustrated. One day I was thinking about this. I thought, 'Have I achieved what I ought to have achieved by now? Should I by now be more successful, be earning more money, be well known, have made more of a mark ... ?' As I asked the Lord about it I felt He gave me a picture. It was of me as a pipe out of which was flowing gushing water, and I felt the Lord saying to me, 'That is what I want you to be – a channel – that is your identity and your function for me.' It gave me a sense of peace and contentment. I realised I didn't have to strive to *be* someone or something, but just be available as a channel through which the Lord could flow. And the more I am yielded to Him the greater the flow of water. Sometimes the channel is blocked by selfishness; the dirt of sin in my life, or the clogging mud of fear; but if I allow Him to sweep all those away, the water can flow on freely.

Every Christian can be used in this way. It has nothing to do with education, talent, wealth, ability – just availability. How available are you, am I, to the Lord for His use, wherever, whenever, however?

CHRIST'S COMMISSION

Before Jesus returned to heaven He told His disciples, 'All authority in heaven and on earth has been given to me. Therefore go and make disciples of all nations...' (Matt. 28:18-19). This commission to the disciples is also a commission to us. If it had been heeded and obeyed by every disciple, the whole world would have been evangelised by now. Jesus also told His disciples where they were to begin this work and how far they should carry the Gospel. '... you will be my witnesses in Jerusalem, and in all Judea and Samaria, and to the ends of the earth' (Acts 1:8). Begin at home and spread out even to the ends of the earth – wherever you go, be a witness.

WITNESSES AT JERUSALEM

We thought earlier about using our homes, entertaining and reaching out to others where we live. Certainly that is where we need to begin. Sometimes it seems harder to witness to friends and family, because they know us so well. But as we choose to co-operate with God in making the necessary changes in our lives it will be noticed and questions will be asked. It is true to say that if we cannot witness at home and to our friends, moving to a place where we are not known is not going to make a lot of difference, though we may like to think it would.

THE UTTERMOST PARTS OF THE EARTH

The question has often been asked, 'What would happen to the mission field if it wasn't for the single man or woman (the latter especially)?' As we said in Chapter 4, the single person is free to pursue the things of God first and is often free to go to places where a married person couldn't go and do things which a married person couldn't do.

It should be a great concern and burden to us that so much of the world is as yet unevangelised. In 1976 there were 4,019 million people in the world. Of those, 2,800 million were non-Christians. That means that nearly 2,000 years after Christ gave His commission, less than half the world has responded to the claims of Christ – and many have never even heard. Communism and Islam are growing in strength while Western Christianity appears to be getting weaker, through compromise with the world and, often, uncertainty of belief. We have become like the trumpet giving out an uncertain sound and consequently few are preparing for the battle (1 Cor. 14:8AV).

I am not suggesting that all single Christians should be involved full time in mission abroad or in this country. Of course not. But I am saying that first of all we should be aware of the world's need and be much in prayer – informed prayer. Second, wherever we are and whatever work we do, we should be aware that we are to be witnesses for the Lord to our friends, family and colleagues – in fact taking every opportunity to witness. And third, we should be open and available to the Lord for Him to put us where He knows we can best be used.

GOD'S CALL

Sometimes people are terrified at the thought of mission work and are fearful of committing themselves wholly to the

Lord in case he asks them to go abroad as missionaries. One of Satan's greatest ploys, from the beginning of time, has been to try and make us doubt the goodness and power of God. He will seek to warn us away from committing ourselves fully to the Lord lest He ask something of us that we shall not be able to do. Satan knows, even if we don't, that that is untrue. God will never ask us to do anything without giving us the strength and, I should say, the desire to do it: not perhaps at the beginning, but as we surrender to His will, often we find our desires have changed.

For the first few years of my Christian life I told the Lord that I would do whatever He wanted me to do, and in my case that included going to the mission field. There was only one thing I requested the Lord not to ask of me. And that was that I should become a nurse. The whole idea terrified me. Hospitals, sick people, blood were all anathema to me. My next thought was, 'I'm sure God won't ask me, anyway, because He knows I'd be a hopeless nurse, impractical – just not my style.' You can therefore imagine my horror, first of all, when I became aware that God was asking this of me, and then my surprise to find that my desires in this area were changing. I suddenly found myself wanting to become a nurse. At first it was not easy and I still had some severe struggles, but when I at last completely gave in to the Lord's pressure, I not only found that I enjoyed my training but also that the Lord enabled me not to be a hopeless nurse after all.

You might ask, 'How did you know God was calling you to be a nurse?' There are many ways that God can make His will known to us. In my case it began through seeking counsel concerning my future from a mature and wise Christian who knew me well. When she suggested nursing, I was horrified and tried to forget that she said it. But as I continued praying about the future I became increasingly aware in my heart that this was the way God was leading me. And when I began to push some doors and to apply for training God's leading became very clear and I knew it was right to go ahead.

Looking back on the whole experience now, I can see that God took me into nursing training because he had much work to do on my character. I learned some valuable lessons, not only of a practical nature but also in the areas both of learning to be under authority, and of being in a position of authority and responsibility. Having been through Bible College by then, the whole experience of nursing training thrust me out into the world again: a world of suffering, and one in which I received many knocks and had some of my corners rubbed off. We all need this experience and there are many different ways in which we may receive it, but I know that for me nursing was a very valuable training towards that end.

Sometimes I have heard Christians say, and it has saddened me, that if a certain course of action looked good and attractive to them then God would certainly not lead them in that direction simply because they desired it so much. In other words, they see God as a killjoy bent on denying us everything that we desire. How unlike the Psalmist who said, 'Delight yourself in the Lord and *he will give you the desires of your heart*' (Ps. 37:4) (my italics).

I have found in my own life that most of my guidance has come through the Lord's fulfilling a desire in my heart. When God called me from nursing to work with the Navigators I had been praying and hoping that this would happen for some time. Because of the particular way the Navigators are set up in their training and recruiting structure, you don't apply to them as you would most other organisations, but you are invited to join the staff. I had been, of my own volition, attending their Bible studies and had asked one of their staff members to disciple me, but from then on the initiative was theirs as far as gaining a new staff member was concerned. All I could do was to pray. And as I did this, although there was pressure on me from other quarters to serve the Lord in a different area, my desire to work with the Navigators intensified. When the time came that I needed to know what to do next in my life the invitation from the Navigators came.

I am not saying this always happens. I illustrated that fact by giving my experience of being called into nursing against my will. But what I am saying is that when we come to know the Lord's will He'll often put desires into our hearts that He later fulfils, resulting in deep satisfaction.

FINDING GOD'S WILL

This often poses a problem to Christians. 'How can I find out what God wants me to do with my life?' they ask. So – how does God make His will known to us? I believe God reveals His will to us in a number of ways: through the Scriptures, through prayer, through circumstances, through the help and advice of mature and wise Christians and through a deep peace and assurance in our own hearts. I am speaking now of guidance to a Christian who has surrendered to the Lord and sincerely desires to know and do God's will. Romans 12:1-2 (AV) tells us that we are to surrender ourselves to God as a living sacrifice and in so doing we shall come to know God's 'good, and acceptable, and perfect, will'.

When I said that we received guidance from God's word, I didn't of course mean that something in the Scriptures told me specifically to enter nursing, join the Navigators or go to America. Of course not. But as I was studying and seeking to obey God's word, certain truths seemed to stand out to me which, together with the other means of guidance mentioned earlier, all seemed to point in the same direction. For example, when I first became aware of the type of ministry the Navigators were engaged in I felt my heart being drawn to it as I saw the need for more follow-up after evangelism and more discipleship training. At that particular time not so much of either ministry was going on. So I told God that if he ever wanted to use me in such ministry I would be available

to Him for that work. It was not until a few years later that
God answered that prayer. In the meantime I had learned
more about the work, had experienced what it was to be
discipled myself by another, had received counsel from more
mature and wiser Christians about my future, and had begun
to discover what gifts God had given me. Then I came across
these words, 'And the things that thou hast heard of me
among many witnesses, the same commit thou to faithful
men, who shall be able to teach others also' (2 Tim. 2:2 AV).
This is the core and centre of the Navigator work and God
made it real and personal to me.

Talking over your future with someone who knows you
well, and who is a praying Christian, can be a very valuable
and helpful thing to do. Often another person will be able to
see things more objectively whereas we can be caught up
with our emotions. They may have noticed gifts you did not
know you had. On the other hand, we may think we have a
gift or a special aptitude until we meet another person who is
more objective and sees things in quite a different light and
helpfully shares that with us, preventing us from going into
something for which, perhaps, we are totally unsuited. In
Christian work there are so many square pegs in round
holes!

Circumstances are also a means of guidance. It is
sometimes true that circumstances may be against us and yet
God leads us on in spite of them. But usually circumstances
prove a helpful guide. I heard of a young man who was
having great difficulty in choosing which of several Bible
colleges he should attend. Finally someone asked him if he
had carefully studied all the brochures giving details of each
college. He admitted that he had not and set about this task.
At the end he discovered that with his qualifications there
was only one of the colleges that would accept him. And so
without further ado he applied and was accepted. His
guidance wasn't really so difficult after all! God will often
guide us through opening or closing doors. Another time in

my life when I was faced with a major decision concerning my future, as all the 'lights seemed green' I went ahead and said 'Yes' to this particular job, praying that if it were not right God would close the door. And there would have been ample opportunity for Him to do that. But He kept the door open and I went through it.

Someone once said, 'Never doubt in the darkness what God has told you in the light.' When it comes to guidance I think that is a valuable lesson to remember. Sometimes after we have followed what we felt to be the Lord's leading and it has been confirmed along the lines I have suggested and all is signed and settled, we find ourselves assailed by appalling doubts. 'Is this just my desire?' 'Did I misinterpret what the Lord has been saying?' At such times I suggest you go back over all that happened. How did you receive guidance in the first place? What actually led you to make the decision? If at that time you felt it was absolutely right and you had peace, then stick with it. Satan will always try to upset you and cause you to go back on God's will. Withstand him and the sin of unbelief which he wants you to fall into. God never promised that when we do His will it will be easy and turn out to be a bed of roses. But He does promise to be with us and to give us the strength to do all that He asks of us.

CELIBACY AS A CALLING

In Matthew 19 Jesus says that there are some people who have chosen to be single for the sake of the kingdom of God. Paul continues this thought in 1 Corinthians 7 by pointing out the fact that those who are single can give their time and attention more readily to the things of God. The married man or woman must put first the concerns and welfare of their spouse and family, while the single person is free to give himself wholly to the work of God.

I think in our present day this is a very important

consideration. Many feel that the second coming of Christ is imminent. The tide of evil seems to be swelling as does the threat of persecution for those standing for morality and righteousness. In some countries this is not a threat but a long-standing reality – and has been so for many years. It has been said that there have already been more Christian martyrs in the twentieth century than any other time in history. And in all this there are thousands who have never even heard of Christ and His claim on their lives. What are we doing about it?

What a challenge there is to the single person not to feel sorry for themselves but to use the freedom that singleness brings to go out perhaps to places where it would be impossible for a family to live, where one might – for instance – be constantly afraid to bring up children, and serve the Lord in a strategic ministry.

One minister, when asked the secret of the outstanding ministry of his church, said that it was because he was single. Of course, it was due also to prayer and the presence and power of the Holy Spirit, but this godly man had given himself unstintingly to his church and congregation in a measure that would have been wrong for a married man with a family.

At the end of that dissertation in Matthew 19 Jesus did say that not all could receive this teaching, but that those who could receive it should do so (v. 12). Let us take that to heart today.

CONCERN FOR ELDERLY PARENTS

I mentioned earlier that as singles we are freer to travel and live abroad than our married friends unless there are elderly parents who need our care. Certainly this is a growing concern today as people are living longer and the whole structure of our society has changed. The extended family is not so much in evidence now as it was when grandparents lived with the family till the end of their days. Today, economically and practically (with smaller homes) this usually is not possible. It would be good to make this a matter of family discussion *before* the need arises and emotions are running high. The *whole* family should be involved not just the single son or daughter. In some cases, where a marriage can stand it and there is a good relationship with the elderly relative, it is far better for them to be with a family, enjoying and being enjoyed by grandchildren, and other family members, than just with one single child who also has to work, look after the home and care for the elderly relative singlehanded – a virtually impossible task. I know of some sad cases where single daughters have been left to bear this burden and other family members have done nothing – not even visited.

There are a number of factors to be considered before bringing an elderly relative into the home. Anyone thinking of doing this might do well to answer some questions.

1. Is it really in that person's best interests or is it to fulfil in other family members a sense of duty? I heard recently of a sad case where the daughter brought her mother from another country where she had lived for many years and had many friends. The daughter felt that her mother needed looking after, and by her, and so, against her mother's wishes she brought her parent back to England and installed her in her home. The mother had no friends and was in unfamiliar surroundings. The daughter, once she had settled her mother, continued leading her very busy social life and consequently saw little of her mother even though she was living under the same roof.

2. Is there a compatible relationship? Or is there an extreme emotional dependence on the part of the parent which could prove life-sapping for the son or daughter? If the

relationship is not for the most part compatible (certainly
there will always be differences, but I am talking about deep-
rooted incompatibilities which could cause great dis-
harmony in a household), or if there is too much emotional
dependence, then an alternative should be sought. Much is
being done by the state and various organisations to provide
good care. Particularly if and when medical care is needed,
this is an alternative that should be carefully and prayerfully
looked into. Many older people that I have spoken to have
said that they would not want to live with their children.
They covet their independence and it has usually been found
to be best for them to be in their own homes as long as they
possibly can. Thereafter, taking time and trouble to find
good sheltered accommodation or a rest home where family
members will visit regularly and as often as possible, and
with weekends away with the family at their home being
offered, an elderly relative can still feel wanted, part of the
family and included without also feeling a burden.

We are told to honour our parents and this we should
certainly do. We owe them the gift of life and in many cases
much sacrificial love and devotion on their part. So it is
important, as they get older, that we see that the best possible
care is provided for them, and that we as sons and daughters
give them all the love and care that we can. However, the
Lord Jesus also challenged us that our love for Him should
transcend that of our love for our parents (Luke 14:26-7). Of
course, the Lord was not telling us literally to 'hate' our
parents, but that our love for Him and willingness to obey
Him, whatever the cost, should take first place. In some
cases this will mean a sacrifice both on our part and on the
part of our parents – who may have to 'give us up' to the
mission field abroad, for example.

One missionary-society leader told me of the problems
they were experiencing in their mission because of the
numbers of single women missionaries who were leaving the

field to come home to look after their parents. Single men missionaries have done this, too. By the time the parent dies, the missionary was either too old or too worn out to return. I have even heard of a case where the daughter caring for her parents died before they did. On the other hand, I know of a single woman in a very busy travelling and teaching ministry who was told by her married brother that he and other family members had discussed the matter and decided that because of the strategic work of the Lord that she was doing, when the parents became too old to look after themselves he and his family would take them in so that this sister would not have to interrupt her work for God. Oh, for more families like that! I should also like to urge older people with children not to fall into the way of thinking that your children owe you something and therefore they must give up their work and their life for you when you get old. You have raised them to be independent and make a living for themselves, and you should be justifiably proud if this is what they are doing. They may want to care for you personally, but may not be able to do so. Accept that and the love and concern they try to show you in other ways. Don't make it any harder for them than it is already if they are not able to give you a home with them.

GIVE TO RECEIVE

I don't believe we have begun to plumb the depths of all that God has for us if we will only allow Him to show us. 'For since the beginning of the world men have not heard, nor perceived by the ear, neither hath the eye seen, O God, beside thee, what he hath prepared for him that waiteth for him' (Isa. 64:4 AV).

What has God prepared for us? What does He want to do for us? There is so much that we shall never know more than a fraction of in this life, but even what we can know is wonderful. Of one thing I am certain – God desires that we consciously experience an ever-deepening companionship with Him. What an unbelievable privilege that is.

While writing this book I was able to take a belated summer holiday on the sun-soaked island of Cyprus, staying with some dear friends. In the middle of my time with them they had to take off to the mountains for their church weekend retreat. Knowing that I was largely engaged in conference work they very kindly booked me into a beach hotel to enjoy the sun and some relaxation. Sometimes, being on one's own in a strange hotel can be a lonely experience, but I went wanting to meet with the Lord as well as to enjoy the sunshine and pleasant surroundings. I found myself spending much time reading, praying and listening to God and that made it a great highlight of a very happy holiday.

One morning there, as I was reflecting on the reality of friendship with God, I praised Him for three wonderful truths.

1. Unlike a human friendship, my friendship with God would never be terminated by death. God never dies and my death will only result in my being in His visible presence.

2. My friendship with the Lord will never be affected by a geographical move. How many of us have had the sorrow of saying goodbye to close friends when either they or we have left to go to another country or another place many miles away, knowing that we may not see them again at least for many years. God never moves and wherever in the world I may go, He is with me.

3. The third thing that can mar a human friendship is misunderstanding, jealousy and lack of forgiveness. I can react to a friend in these ways and spoil the relationship, or, more difficult still, he or she may react to me in these ways and refuse to be reconciled. So a lovely friendship can end in bitterness.

With God I can feel perfectly safe in knowing that He loves

me and never changes. 'I am the Lord, I change not' (Mal. 3:6 AV). If a break in fellowship occurs it's on my side, and I can restore fellowship by repentance and coming back to God.

As I realised these wonderful truths I sang praises to God out loud in my room.

The Lord is real and He wants us to know the reality of His companionship. Allow Him to comfort you and through His word and the consciousness of His presence. Sometimes I can feel the Lord putting His arms around me almost as really as a human person.

Sometimes the Lord allows us to go through a period of dryness and darkness to test and strengthen us. In these times, once we have ascertained that there is no known and unconfessed sin in our lives, let us accept it from Him, hard though it is, realising that He knows what He is doing and there is always light at the end of the tunnel. Times like this, rightly received, make us stronger in our faith.

God wants us to enjoy a life of fulfilment in finding our true identity and security in Him, beyond and above our circumstances. As we have seen, this will be achieved through our personal and growing knowledge of Him, and through being available to Him to use us as He pleases. He knows how best and most creatively our lives can be lived.

THE LOCUST YEARS

Jacqui Williams with David Porter

A chance encounter in a San Francisco bus station introduced Jacqui Williams to a community that was to change her life. Instead of going home, Jacqui, a young British Christian on holiday in the States, became a member of the Unification Church. In less than three months, she was convinced that the Revd Sun Myung Moon was the Messiah.

Jacqui's dedication – and success – were astonishing. Within two years, she was top fund-raiser for the 'Moonies', following a punishing schedule of hard sell and mission work that took her all over the United States and Canada. But when disillusionment and doubt set in, friends were at hand to point the way to a new life of true freedom, acceptance and love.

Jacqui Williams is now an active member of her local church and a primary school teacher in Bracknell, Berkshire.

David Porter is a freelance writer and journalist. He is the author of many books, including *Children at Risk*.

SPLIT IMAGE

Anne Atkins

Men and women are made in the image of God but that image is distorted in a fallen world. Not only are people cut off from God's intended best for them, but often they are split into competing sexual roles.

Anne Atkins encourages Christians to come to the Bible with a fresh mind to discover God's intention in creating male and female, and draws some challenging and surprising conclusions. Men and women are equal, different and interdependent, and both sexes will be challenged by *Split Image* to pursue the true outworking of this relationship.

It is a superb first book, forceful, well-researched, bold, unconventional and in places breathtaking.'

Michael Green

This book explodes so many of the preconceptions people have about what the Bible says about relationships between the sexes.'

Elaine Storkey

I disagreed with something on nearly every page, and still devoured, loved and immediately started recommending the book.'

Veronica Zundel, *Third Way*

Anne Atkins is an actress, and lives in London with her husband and three children.